ERIC CLAPTON

THE NEW VISUAL DOCUMENTARY BY MARC ROBERTY

OMNIBUS PRESS
LONDON · NEW YORK · SYDNEY

© 1990 Omnibus Press
(A Division of Book Sales Limited)

First published © 1986 Omnibus Press

Edited by Chris Charlesworth
Original Art Direction by Mike Bell
Cover designed by Lisa Pettibone
Book designed by Laurence Bradbury
Picture research by Valerie Boyd & Paul Giblin

ISBN 0.7119.2223.3
Order No. OP43579

Exclusive distributors:

Book Sales Limited,
8/9 Frith Street, London W1V 5TZ, UK.

Music Sales Corporation,
225 Park Avenue South,
New York, NY 10003, USA.

Music Sales Pty Limited,
120 Rothschild Avenue,
Rosebery, NSW 2018, Australia.

To the Music Trade only:

Music Sales Limited,
8/9 Frith Street, London W1V 5TZ, UK.

Typeset by Capital Setters.
Printed in Scotland by Scotprint Limited,
Musselburgh.

Author's note:
Hello and thank you to Joe McMichael, Bob Craig,
Mike Swain, Simon Bell, Mal Barker, Stewart
Pearsall, Carol Norris and Virginia Lohle.

This edition of my book is dedicated to myself!
Marc Roberty, June 1990.

A catalogue record for this book is available
from The British Library.

Title page: Jeff Mayer/Starfile

INTRODUCTION

Eric Patrick Clapton was born on March 30, 1945, at the home of his grandparents, Rose and Jack Clapp, a modest terraced house on The Green in Ripley, Surrey. He was the illegitimate son of Patricia Molly Clapton, who was unmarried, and Edward Fryer, a Canadian soldier stationed in England. After the war Edward Fryer returned to a wife in Canada and thus dropped out of Eric's life forever. Pat Clapton later married a Canadian soldier called Frank McDonald and moved on to Germany and, later, Canada, and young Eric was raised by his grandparents in Ripley. It is an area of the English Home Counties for which Eric has retained an abiding affection, and to this day he lives within a short drive of his birthplace.

From the age of five, Eric attended Ripley Church of England Primary School. At first he appeared to be a bright child, well capable of passing the then all important 11-plus examination and going on to grammar school, but this proved not to be the case and instead he went to St Bede's Secondary Modern at Send, near Woking. Here he showed a natural talent for art and at 14 he was transferred to Hollyfield Road School, Surbiton, which housed the junior department of Kingston College of Art. Two years later he moved on to Kingston Art College proper to study graphic design.

In the meantime Eric had discovered the guitar. His first guitar, a 13th birthday present from Rose and Jack Clapp, was a £14 acoustic from Bell's music shop in Kingston, and before long almost all his waking hours were spent mastering the instrument. It accompanied him on the daily bus journey to Kingston and was the principle reason why he was asked to leave Art School at 16. His first paid employment was as a casual labourer and as a temporary postman over Christmas 1961.

Eric's earliest musical leanings developed into areas more demanding than the current 'pop' music of the day. He became interested in authentic American blues and listened in admiration to records by such black US performers

as Big Bill Broonzy, Muddy Waters, Howlin' Wolf and, most crucially, Robert Johnson, the legendary bluesman from Mississippi who was said to have sold his soul to the devil in exchange for a musical virtuosity that inspired awe-struck envy in his peers. Johnson's mysterious early death, allegedly at the hands of a jealous husband, added credence and fascination to the legend.

Such colourful tales of errant bluesmen from the past might likely have entranced young Eric as he struggled to emulate the tormented emotional performances of these American mentors on his second guitar, a £100 Kay electric. Thus equipped, he joined his first band The Roosters after an invitation from their guitarist Tom McGuinness whose girlfriend attended Kingston Art College and who had observed Eric practising during lunch breaks. As well as McGuinness and Clapton, The Roosters included Ben Palmer (piano), Terry Brennan (vocals) and Robin Mason (drums). When Eric joined McGuinness switched to bass.

The Roosters stayed together for the first six months of 1963, operating around the Richmond area playing rhythm and blues numbers like 'Hoochie Coochie Man' and 'Boom Boom'. Unlike Eric, most of their members had 'day' jobs and to them the band was a secondary occupation. They played a couple of opening shows at the Marquee Club in London but disbanded through a mixture of apathy and lack of outside encouragement.

Eric and Tom McGuinness then briefly joined The Engineers, a band put together to back Casey Jones, one time leader of a Liverpool band called The Casanovas who had since deserted their singer and rechristened themselves The Big Three. The gig lasted a month.

Eric Clapton's next band was to bring him to the attention of a far wider public. He met them at the Crown pub in Kingston, Surrey, and was invited to enlist after making a disparaging remark about their guitarist Paul Samwell-Smith. Their name was The Yardbirds.

3

1963

OCTOBER 1963

Eric rehearses with The Yardbirds at the Great Western pub in Richmond. It is fair to say that Eric was musically superior to the others in the band as well as being very aware of fashion. The band comprises Jim McCarty (drums), Chris Dreja (guitar and vocals), Paul Samwell-Smith (bass), and Keith Relf (vocals and harp).

They have no hesitation in offering the position to Eric and proceed to tour the R & B circuit in and around London: The Palais in Wimbledon, the Toby Jug in Tolworth, the Ricky Tick in Windsor, The Crawdaddy in Richmond, the Cooks Ferry Inn in Edmonton, the Plaza Ballroom in Guildford. The Yardbirds also enter R. G. Jones studios in Surrey to cut demos of 'Boom Boom', 'Honey In Your Hips' and 'Baby What's Wrong'.

Right: The Yardbirds, 1964. Left to right: Paul Samwell Smith, Keith Relf, Jim McCarty, Eric Clapton, Chris Dreja. (Dezo Hoffman)

Right, above and below: Eric totes different Fender guitars during his stint with The Yardbirds. (Dezo Hoffman)

NOVEMBER 1963

The Yardbirds enter Olympic Studios, Barnes, to record their first single 'I Wish You Would'/'A Certain Girl'.

7,8

Crawdaddy Club, Richmond.

20

Ricky Tick, Windsor. The Yardbirds started playing R & B style but very quickly develop a more 'pop' approach. Eric, a blues purist, is not entirely satisfied with this, particularly as they are asked to back American bluesman Sonny Boy Williamson.

Opposite page: Eric's first appearance on vinyl. The Yardbirds pose to promote their debut single 'I Wish You Would', released July 1964.

1963/64

Above, right: The Yardbirds pose beside The Serpentine in Hyde Park, London. Left to right: Keith Relf, Paul Samwell Smith, Chris Dreja, Eric Clapton, Jim McCarty. (Dezo Hoffman)

Below, right: Nineteen-year-old Eric. (Dezo Hoffman)

Eric Clapton: **We didn't know how to back him up. It was frightening, really, because this man was real and we weren't. He wasn't very tolerant, either. I had to almost relearn how to play. It taught me a lot; it taught me the value of that music.**

This is clearly demonstrated on the live LP 'Sonny Boy Williamson and The Yardbirds' recorded at the Crawdaddy Club on the 8th December 1963.

JANUARY 1964

The Yardbirds spend most of the year touring the clubs.

3
The Marquee, London.

10
The Marquee, London.

17
The Marquee, London.

20
Toby Jug Hotel, Tolworth.

24
The Marquee, London.

31
The Marquee, London.

FEBRUARY 1964

7
The Marquee, London.

14
The Marquee, London.

21
The Marquee, London.

28
First Rhythm and Blues Festival, Birmingham Town Hall. Part of this show was released as 'Rock Generation Series, Vol. V' BYG 522705.

MARCH 1964

The Yardbirds enter Olympic Studios, Barnes, to record their

second single 'Good Morning Little School Girl'/'I Ain't Got You'.

1
Crawdaddy Club, Richmond.

6
Telephone House, Wimbledon.

13
The Marquee, London. The Yardbirds play just about every night

by now, and they record one of their March Marquee shows for release as the 'Five Live Yardbirds' L.P.

MAY 1964
4
Eric plays his first studio session on two tracks for Otis Spann, 'Pretty Girls Everywhere' and 'Stirs Me Up' alongside Muddy Waters, Ransome Knowling, Willie Smith and Jimmy Page.

22
The Marquee, London.

Left and far left: More shots in Hyde Park. (Pictorial Press)

Below, left: The Yardbirds performing 'For Your Love', their last single on which Eric appeared, before the television cameras. Left to right: Paul Samwell Smith, Keith Relf, Chris Dreja, Eric Clapton and Jim McCarty. (SKR Photos/LFI)

FIVE LIVE YARDBIRDS

UK Columbia SX 1677
No US release
Released January 1965

Side One:
1. Too Much Monkey Business
2. I Got Love If You Want It
3. Smokestack Lightnin'
4. Good Morning Little Schoolgirl
5. Respectable
Side Two:
6. Five Long Years
7. Pretty Girl
8. Louise
9. I'm A Man
10. Here 'Tis

1964/65

JUNE 1964

13
Club Norien, London.

26
Northern Jazz Festival, Redcar.

AUGUST 1964

9
Fourth Jazz and Blues Festival, Richmond. Brenda Lee releases 'Be True' as a single. Eric plays on the A side.

DECEMBER 1964

24
Hammersmith Odeon, London, as support act for The Beatles Christmas Show.

The Yardbirds also enter IBC Studios, London, to cut 'For Your Love' as their new single.

Eric had already become disenchanted with The Yardbirds, but the obvious pop sound of 'For Your Love' was really the final straw. The Yardbirds had by now also stopped playing clubs and were doing huge package tours with Gene Vincent, Billy J. Kramer, The Kinks, and The Small Faces to name but a few.

Eric Clapton: **My attitude within the group got really sour, and it was kind of hinted that it would be better for me to leave. 'Cause they'd already been to see Jeff Beck play, and at the time he was far more adaptable than I was. I was withdrawing into myself, becoming intolerable, really dogmatic. So they kind of asked me to leave, and I left and felt a lot better for it.**

MARCH 1965

3
Corn Exchange, Bristol. This is Eric's final show with The Yardbirds.

Keith Relf: **He loves the blues so much I suppose he didn't like it being played badly by a white shower like us.**

Eric wisely decides to take a break and gather his thoughts. He spends some time with his old friend from The Roosters, Ben Palmer, at his home in Oxford, where he gets a call from John Mayall asking him to an audition.

John Mayall: **I'd seen Eric playing before our paths crossed and when I heard that B side of 'For Your Love', it confirmed my belief in his abilities.**

The B side in question was 'Got To Hurry'.

APRIL 1965

Eric joins John Mayall's Bluesbreakers which comprises John Mayall (organ and vocals), Hughie Flint (drums) and John McVie (bass). Eric is now using a Gibson Les Paul, rather than the Fender Telecaster or Gibson 335 which were used in The Yardbirds, giving him a harder sound. Maybe Eric was rebelling against the confines of his previous band, but his playing was the most aggressive on

Right: John Mayall demonstrates percussive techniques to a group of young admirers. (Dezo Hoffman)

any British stage at that time.

In John Mayall he found someone he could relate to, and who also had the best blues record collection in England. Eric plays in the style of Otis Rush, Buddy Guy and Freddie King and found many of their singles in John's collection.

MAY 1965

John Mayall's Bluesbreakers with Eric enter the studio to record tracks for Andrew Oldham's Immediate label with a view to releasing a single. The tracks they record are 'I'm Your Witchdoctor', 'Telephone Blues', and 'On Top Of The World'. The session is produced by Jimmy Page who at the time was one of the top London studio guitarists.

It is probable that Eric also recorded some demos with Jimmy Page at this time which were to surface when both reached the superstar league. These tracks were 'Draggin' My Tail', 'Choker', 'Miles Road', 'Snake Drive', 'Freight Loader', 'West Coast Idea' and 'Tribute to Elmore'. They appeared on Immediate's Anthology Of British Blues Vol. I (IMAL 03/04) and Vol. II (IMAL 05/06) released 1968.

JULY 1965

Eric was obviously happy playing with John, but the constant pressure of playing nightly and travelling in uncomfortable circumstances takes its toll. He decides to take a break from the routine and have some fun.

AUGUST, SEPTEMBER, OCTOBER 1965

Eric lives with Ben Palmer and other friends from Oxford and decides to form a band, The Glands, and tour the world. They comprise Ben Palmer (piano), John Bailey (vocals), Bob Ray (bass), Jake Milton (drums) and Bernie Greenwood (sax).

This wild idea no doubt came about after numerous bottles of wine had been consumed. However, they all pool their money, buy an estate wagon and drive to Greece. They soon realise that they are nobody special, despite the fact they are English and The Beatles are riding

high in the charts along with other R&B bands such as The Kinks. They are given a support slot to a local Greek band who are later involved in a serious road accident in which half of them are killed. This puts Eric in the awkward position of having to play with both bands and it isn't long before he realises that the manager of the club is not prepared to let him go. By this time the rest of the English band were fired and the manager is holding Eric's prize Gibson Les Paul and amplifier to make sure he doesn't leave. Ben Palmer and Eric decide that the only way out is through trickery; Eric asks the club owner's permission to take his guitar to get it re-strung. He agrees and, needless to say, that was the last he saw of Eric.

NOVEMBER 1965

Eric returns to England and rejoins John Mayall's Bluesbreakers which now includes Jack Bruce (bass), albeit for a short period as Jack joins Manfred Mann in December 1965 and John McVie is brought back in.

Jack Bruce: There was a great thing between me and Eric even then. He knew of me before. He'd seen me with Graham (Bond) a couple of times and he dug my playing.

Eric Clapton: There was something creative there. Most of what we were doing with Mayall was imitating the records we got, but Jack had something else – he had no reverence for what we were doing, and so he was composing new parts as he went along playing.

Left: John Mayall in 1965. (Dezo Hoffman)

1966

BLUESBREAKERS WITH ERIC CLAPTON

UK Decca SKL4804
US London PS 492
Released July 1966

Side One:
1. All Your Love
2. Hideaway
3. Little Girl
4. Another Man
5. Double Crossing
6. What'd I Say
Side Two:
7. Key To Love
8. Parchment Farm
9. Have You Heard
10. Ramblin' On My Mind
11. Steppin' Out
12. It's All Right

Right: Cream follow in the footsteps of The Yardbirds by having their photograph taken in Hyde Park. Left to right: Eric Clapton, Ginger Baker, Jack Bruce. (David Redfern)

JANUARY 1966

Eric and John Mayall are invited to appear on a 'Champion' Jack Dupree session with Mike Vernon producing. The three tracks featuring Eric are 'Calcutta Blues', 'Shim-Sham-Shimmy' and 'Third Degree'.

FEBRUARY 1966

Mike Vernon wants to record Eric and John Mayall together as a duo and release it on his independent label. They agree and, at Wessex Studios in Soho, record 'Lonely Years' and 'Bernard Jenkins'.

Mike Vernon: **We did it straight mono, one microphone stuck up in the middle of the studio, just piano, voice and a guitar, and to this day it's the only record I've ever made that sounds as if it was made in Chicago.**

John Mayall likes Mike Vernon's production and asks him to produce his new LP as soon as he is signed up again with Decca.

MARCH 1966

One off studio band comprising Eric (guitar), Jack Bruce (bass), Paul Jones (harmonica), Pete York (drums) and Stevie Winwood (keyboards) record three tracks, 'I Want To Know', 'Crossroads', and 'Steppin Out', for Elektra. They are known as The Powerhouse. Quite how this all came about is not documented. However, Eric would often play with The Spencer Davis Group as well as other R & B groups at that time so it would not have been unusual to record a similar studio jam.

It is also around this time that John Mayall's Bluesbreakers enter Decca's West Hampstead Studios to record what is to be one of Eric's finest guitar playing moments on vinyl. Eric insists on playing at stage volume levels which present all sorts of complications for engineer Gus Dudgeon. Eric refuses to compromise and it's fair to say that when the LP was released in August 1966, it was a masterpiece despite any technical problems.

Melody Maker: **No British musicians have ever sounded like this before on record. It is a giant step. It is a credit to John and his musicians.**

Beat Instrumental: **It's Eric Clapton who steals the limelight and no doubt several copies of the album will be sold on the strength of his name.**

It is interesting to note that when the album did come out, it mentioned Eric's name on the front cover: 'John Mayall's Bluesbreakers Featuring Eric Clapton'. This was the only time that Mayall shared billing on an LP cover. But it was all too late.

Eric Clapton: **I don't think there will be room for me here much longer. None of my music is English – it is rooted in Chicago. I represent what is going on in Chicago at the moment, the best I can anyway, because it's difficult to get all the records imported... Anyway I think the only way is to go to America.**

It is clear that Eric is dissatisfied with just copying blues guitar riffs and wants to take it one step further with improvisation. He sees this as a possibility... with Jack Bruce in mind should he form a new band.

MAY, JUNE 1966

The Graham Bond Organisation had been playing the same circuit as The Bluesbreakers and features Ginger Baker on drums who is interested in breaking away and forming a new band due to lack of mass appeal and progress. Ginger had played with Eric once before at one of the Richmond Festivals, and was keen to

Left, above and below: Eric in 1966. (Dezo Hoffman)

jam with him again. This they did quite frequently during this period and they decide to form a band. Eric insists on including Jack Bruce who at the time was with the successful Manfred Mann. All three rehearse secretly for obvious reasons although it is impossible to keep it from the press for long.

Melody Maker: **Groups' group starring Eric Clapton, Jack Bruce and Ginger Baker is being formed... The group say they hope to start playing clubs, ballrooms and theatres in a month's time.**

Robert Stigwood: **They will be called Cream and will be represented by me for agency and management. They will record for my Reaction label and go into the studios next week to cut tracks for their first single. Their début will be at the National Jazz and Blues Festival at Windsor in July, when their single will be released.**

Cream go to Chalk Farm Studios and record 'Wrapping Paper' and 'Cat's Squirrel'.

1966

Far right: Following a visit to his tailors, 1966, Eric takes the vocal for the Ready Steady Go! studio audience. (David Redfern)

Near right: Still at RSG! (Dezo Hoffman)

FRESH CREAM

UK Reaction 593001
US Atco SD 33-206
Released December 1966

Side One:
1. NSU
2. Sleepy Time
3. Dreaming
4. Sweet Wine
5. Spoonful
Side Two:
6. Cat's Squirrel
7. Four Until Late
8. Rollin' And Tumblin'
9. I'm So Glad
10. Toad

JULY 1966

2

Cream play a warm up show at the Twisted Wheel, Manchester.

3

Cream's first official live appearance at the 6th National Jazz and Blues Festival at Windsor.

The tour continues through August playing venues like Cooks Ferry Inn, Edmonton, The Marquee, London, The Cellar Club, Kensington, The Manor Lounge, Stockport, and The Ram Jam Club, Brixton.

The basic Cream set at the time usually consists of the following numbers: 'Cat's Squirrel', 'Lawdy Mama', 'Spoonful', 'Sweet Wine', 'Toad', 'Crossroads', 'NSU', 'Stepping Out' and 'Traintime'. This would be more or less the same set throughout 1966, although the versions would be different in style and length depending how the band were feeling.

SEPTEMBER 1966

Cream record their first LP 'Fresh Cream'.

OCTOBER 1966

Cream continue to tour extensively in such places as The Public Baths, Sutton, Sussex University, The Birdcage, Portsmouth, as well as a historical gig in London.

12

Cream play the Central Polytechnic in London. This was a special gig, in that Jimi Hendrix was introduced to Eric who in turn invited him to jam on 'Killing Floor' with Cream.

Eric Clapton: **He became a soul mate for me and musically, what I wanted to hear.**

Eric, along with Pete Townshend, is frequently seen with Jimi Hendrix in various clubs in London such as The Flamingo. It is fair to say that they both admired Jimi, but they were also checking out the competition.

'Wrapping Paper' backed with 'Cat's Squirrel' released as Cream's first single. A very strange choice indeed.

Eric Clapton: **When we made 'Wrapping Paper' we didn't think it would harm the image and personally I haven't had any real protests. We knew some people would like it and some wouldn't.**

Jack Bruce: **We did it because we didn't want people to put us into a category straight away. We play soft numbers on stage, maybe we'll change it next time.**

NOVEMBER 1966

More touring on the club circuit every night, such as the Town Hall, East Ham, The Marquee, London and Klooks Kleek, West Hampstead (a bootleg of this gig exists) on the 12th.

DECEMBER 1966

'I Feel Free' backed with 'N.S.U.' released as Cream's second single.

'Fresh Cream' also released as Cream's first album.

Eric Clapton: **I am not happy about it as it could have been better. We were working on it so long ago and we have greatly improved since then. I'm not completely happy with the production.**

However, the public disagree and the single makes the top twenty and album the top five.

9

First radio broadcast of live Cream material on Rhythm and Blues Show. Numbers performed: 'Cat's Squirrel', 'Traintime', 'Lawdy Mama', and 'I'm So Glad'.

15

Radio broadcast on *Saturday Club*. Numbers performed: 'Sweet Wine'. 'Stepping Out', and 'Wrapping Paper'. Eric interviewed.

Cream continue to tour extensively throughout December.

Above left: Performing with Cream, 1966. (Nigel Dickson)

Below left: With Jack Bruce, on the set of Ready Steady Go! (Dezo Hoffman)

1966

Top left: (Jan Persson)

Others: Selecting threads with Ginger and Jack. (Pictorial Press)

Opposite page: (Barry Wentzell)

14

1967

Top, right: Cream, with well wishers, leave Heathrow Airport for Los Angeles, August 20, 1967. (BBC)

Far right: On the streets of Soho in 1967. (Dezo Hoffman)

JANUARY 1967
10
Radio broadcast on *Saturday Club*. Numbers performed: 'Four Until Late', 'I Feel Free' and 'N.S.U.'. Eric interviewed.

19
Radio broadcast on *Saturday Club*. Number performed: 'Take It Back'.

FEBRUARY, MARCH 1967
Cream tour France, Holland, Germany and Scandinavia to rave reviews.

MARCH 1967
Cream head off for their first American visit.

25, 26, 27, 28, 29, 30, 31
RKO Theatre, New York.

APRIL 1967
1, 2, 3
RKO Theatre, New York. Cream perform for ten days, five times a day, on Murray The K Show along with various other popular bands of the day: The Who, Lovin' Spoonful, Mitch Ryder and Wilson Pickett.

Ben Palmer (Cream's Road manager): It was a big bill, a lot of acts, and it was supposed to be five shows a day. I think the first curtain was at ten o'clock in the morning – the kids were on holiday – and the last show would go on not far short of midnight, and that was for the supper crowd coming out of the theatres.

After their appearance on the Murray The K Shows, Cream enter Atlantic's New York studio to record their second album 'Disraeli Gears'.

MAY 1967
1
Radio broadcast on *Saturday Club*. Numbers performed: 'Strange Brew', 'Tales Of Brave Ulysses' and 'We're Going Wrong'.

4
Radio broadcast on *Top Gear*, numbers performed: 'Train Time', 'N.S.U.', 'Toad', 'Four Until Late', 'Strange Brew', 'Tales Of Brave Ulysses' and 'We're Going Wrong'.

27
Pembroke College May Ball, Oxford.

29
Auction Hall, Spalding.

JUNE 1967
'Strange Brew' backed with 'Tales Of Brave Ulysses' released as single.

AUGUST 1967
13
7th Jazz and Blues Festival, Windsor. Meanwhile…Robert Stigwood has been working behind the scenes to organize a short US tour for his boys which opened on the West Coast.

20
Whiskey A Go Go, Los Angeles, Ca.

22, 23, 24, 25, 27, 29, 30, 31.
Fillmore West, San Francisco, Ca.

SEPTEMBER 1967
1, 2, 3
Fillmore West, San Francisco, Ca.

Jack Bruce: We'd just been doing three, four, five minute versions of our songs before we went out to San Francisco, and we were very, very nervous because this was something really big for us and also it was almost the first time we had played to a full house. But all these kids had actually come to see us and it was the first time we'd had our own audience on that scale, and they were just shouting things like 'Just play anything...just play...we love you' and stuff, and the whole thing ended up with us just playing these incredibly long improvised things. We became known for that I suppose, and that was how it started, and it was the best time for the group.

Top, left: Ginger, Jack and Eric. (Pictorial Press)

Centre, left: Eric with friends. (Dezo Hoffman)

Bottom, far left: In the audience for a change. (David Redom)

Bottom left: On stage at the NME Poll Winners concert, Wembley, 1967. (Dezo Hoffman)

4, 5, 6

Whiskey A Go Go, Los Angeles, Ca. The tour continues on the East Coast, playing such venues as the Psychedelic Supermarket in Boston and the Village Theatre in New York after which they again enter Atlantic Studios to record 'Wheels Of Fire', at which time Eric also contributes a guitar solo to 'Good To Me As I Am To You' by Aretha Franklin playing alongside Cornell Dupree, Joe South and Jimmy Johnson.

Eric Clapton: We'll be making tracks, and if something appears that's suitable, it may be put out as a single. But we won't allocate any special time to making singles now.

1967

Right: Psychedelia exerts an influence over Cream. (Karl Ferris)

Far right, below: On stage with Cream. (Relay Photos)

Opposite page: (Relay Photos)

DISRAELI GEARS

UK Reaction 593003
US Atco 33-232
Released November 1967

Side One:
1. Strange Brew
2. Sunshine Of Your Love
3. World Of Pain
4. Dance The Night Away
5. Blue Condition
Side Two:
6. Tales Of Brave Ulysses
7. Swlabr
8. We're Going Wrong
9. Outside Woman Blues
10. Take It Back
11. Mother's Lament

OCTOBER 1967
On their return to the UK, Cream play a short English tour including a memorable performance on…

29
Saville Theatre, London.

NOVEMBER 1967
2
Radio broadcast *Top Gear*. Numbers performed: 'Take It Back', 'Outside Woman Blues' and 'Sunshine Of Your Love'.

6
Silver Blades, Streatham.

9-14
Cream tour Scandinavia.

15
Radio Broadcast on *Top Gear*.

23
Club A Go Go, Newcastle-upon-Tyne.

24
Central Pier, Morecambe.

28
The Marquee, London. Cream's second LP 'Disraeli Gears' released during November. A great record which captures the feeling of '67.

Eric Clapton: We used Atlantic's New York studios. It's done quicker there, we get a better sound and there's a really hip engineer…one of the best in America.

The engineer in question is, of course, Tom Dowd.

Tom Dowd: On 'Disraeli Gears', I remember Eric using a wah wah pedal and a pair of Marshall stacks, the sound was mainly just the Marshalls turned all the way up. They recorded at ear-shattering level.

DECEMBER 1967
1
Top Rank, Brighton.

3
Radio broadcast on *Top Gear*. Number performed: 'Born Under A Bad Sign'.

1968

Top, near right: (Jan Persson)

Top, far right: In the dressing room. (LFI)

Below, far right: (David Redfern)

Bottom: Backstage with Cream. (Chris Walter)

JANUARY 1968
14
Radio broadcast on *Top Gear*. Numbers performed: 'Swalbr', 'Politician', 'Steppin Out' and 'Blue Condition'.

FEBRUARY 1968
Cream begin their longest US tour which opens on 29th February and closes on 15th June. Some of the dates:

29
Fillmore West, San Francisco, Ca.

MARCH 1968
1, 2, 3
Winterland, San Francisco, Ca.

7, 8, 9, 10
Winterland, San Francisco, Ca.

16, 17
Shrine Auditorium, Los Angeles, Ca.

18
Convention Centre, Anaheim, Ca.

20
Eric busted on marijuana charge alongside Neil Young, Richie Furay and Jim Messina.

21
Beloit College, Beloit, Wi.

22
Butler University, Butler, In.

23
Brown University, Providence, R.I.

27
Staples High School, Westport, Ct.

29
Hunter College Auditorium, New York, N.Y.

30
Dallas, Tx.

Left: On tour with Cream in Scandinavia. (Jan Persson x 3)

Bottom left: (John Shepherd)

Overleaf
Left: On the streets of Soho. (Alec Byrne/Relay Photos)

Right: With an elderly admirer in Hyde Park. (Alex Byrne/Relay Photos)

1968

WHEELS OF FIRE

UK Polydor 583031/2
US Atco SD 2-700
Released August 1968

Side One:
1. White Room
2. Sitting On Top Of The World
3. Passing The Time
4. As You Said
Side Two:
5. Pressed Rat And Warthog
6. Politician
7. Those Were The Days
8. Born Under A Bad Sign
9. Deserted Cities Of The Heart
Side Three:
10.Crossroads
11.Spoonful
Side Four:
12.Traintime
13.Toad

Right: Performing with Cream at their Farewell Concert at London's Royal Albert Hall, November 26, 1968. (Barry Plummer)

31
Houston, Tx.

APRIL 1968
5
Back Bay Theater, Boston, Mass.

6
Commodore Ballroom, Lowell, Mass.

7
Eastman Theater, Rochester, N.Y.

8
Capitol Theater, Ottawa, Ont. Cream interrupt their tour for a ten day break. Pressures mount and rumours of a split are reported in the music press.

Eric Clapton: **All the rumours are denied. I'm happy with the group, although needless to say there has been strain. We've been doing two and a half months of one-nighters and that is the hardest I've ever worked in my life. Financially and popularity wise we're doing unbelievably well in America.**

MAY 1968
Cream's 4th single released: 'Anyone For Tennis' backed with 'Pressed Rat And Warthog'.

12
Music Hall, Cleveland, Oh.

25
Civic Auditorium, San Jose, Ca.

JUNE 1986
15
Oakdale Music Theatre, Wallingford, Ct. After the tour ends it is announced that Cream will break up after a farewell tour of both England and America.

Eric Clapton: **I've been on the road seven years and I'm going on a big holiday.**

Robert Stigwood: **Cream are going to follow their individual musical policies.**

It is fair to say that Cream ignored England and their fans' reaction was one of anger and sadness.

Melody Maker: **Goodbye Eric, Jack and Ginger. We dug your sound, but you kicked us in the teeth.**

Cream's set at this time would usually run in the following order: 'Tales Of Brave Ulysses', 'Sunshine Of Your Love', 'N.S.U.', 'I'm Sitting On Top Of The World', 'Steppin' Out', 'Traintime' and 'Toad'.

AUGUST 1968
'Wheels Of Fire', a double album, released. One LP is from studio sessions while the other is live from the Fillmore West in San Francisco.

By this time, however, Eric was becoming influenced by Bob Dylan's backing musicians, The Band.

Eric Clapton: **I think this music will influence a lot of people. Everybody I have played it to has flipped. The Band is releasing an album called 'Music From Big Pink' by the group. Since I heard all this stuff all my values have changed. I think it has probably influenced me.**

Cream take a three month break before undertaking their farewell tour.

SEPTEMBER 1968
Cream's 5th single released: 'Sunshine Of Your Love' backed with 'Swlabr'. It reaches number 5 in the American charts which shows how popular they were over there thanks to heavy touring; but it only just reaches the UK top thirty.

During this three month period Eric develops a close friendship with George Harrison and as a result

begins playing on his sessions as well as various Apple artists such as Billy Preston, Doris Troy, Jackie Lomax and, of course, The Beatles at their Apple Studios in Savile Row, London.

Although Eric has been involved in various sessions before (Brenda Lee and Aretha Franklin as well as various bluesmen), this period is the real start of his involvement as a major guest artist which continues to this day.

OCTOBER 1968

Cream start their 15 show farewell tour of America. The set performed at this time would usually run in the following order: 'White Room', 'Politician', 'I'm So Glad', 'Sittin' On Top Of The World', 'Sunshine Of Your Love', 'Deserted Cities Of The Heart', 'Toad', and 'Spoonful'.

4
Albuquerque, NM.

7
Civic Opera House, Chicago, Ill.

11
Arena, New Haven, Ct.

13
Coliseum, Chicago, Ill.

18
The Forum, Los Angeles, Ca.

23
Coliseum, Chicago, Ill.

25
Memorial Auditorium, Dallas, Tx.

NOVEMBER 1968
1
Spectrum, Philadelphia, Pa.

2
Madison Square Garden, New York, N.Y. Cream receive a platinum record for 'Wheels Of Fire', representing $2 million worth of sales. The award is made on-stage at this show.

3
Civic Centre, Baltimore, Md. Last US show.

26
Royal Albert Hall, London. Cream perform to two sold out houses. The set for their second and final ever gig runs as follows: 'White Room', 'Politican', 'I'm So Glad', 'Sittin' On Top Of The World', 'Crossroads', 'Toad', 'Spoonful', 'Sunshine Of Your Love' and 'Steppin' Out'. The second and final show was filmed by Tony Palmer for broadcast by the BBC early in 1969.

Eric Clapton: **We haven't played here for — well I don't know how long — over a year, and I had no idea we were so popular. I was amazed we played to such full houses. I didn't think anybody would remember us...it was really a fine evening for me, and I felt very excited.**

Eric plays a Gibson Firebird for the first show and a Gibson ES 335 for the second.

November also sees the release of The Beatles' double album, 'The

Above: The view from the audience at the Royal Albert Hall Farewell show. (Barry Plummer)

1968/69

White Album'. Eric plays on 'While My Guitar Gently Weeps' and George Harrison releases his 'Wonderwall' album on which Eric plays on 'Ski-ing'.

DECEMBER 1968

Cream record their last three studio cuts for their 'Goodbye' LP, 'Badge' on which George Harrison plays rhythm guitar, 'What A Bringdown' and 'Doing That Scrapyard Thing'.

10, 11

Intertel Studios, Wembley. Eric takes part in the 'Rock And Roll Circus' film, an entertainment extravaganza put on by The Rolling Stones. Artists who appear during the two day period include The Who, Taj Mahal, Jethro Tull, The Rolling Stones, and a one off group consisting of Eric (lead guitar), John Lennon (vocals and rhythm guitar), Mitch Mitchell (drums) and Keith Richards (bass).

They perform two songs, the first being 'Yer Blues' followed by an instrumental where they are joined by Yoko Ono for vocal improvisations and virtuoso violinist Ivry Gitlis.

December also marks the end of Traffic. Eric and Stevie Winwood begin to jam together with the possibility of a joint venture at a later date should their ideas materialize.

JANUARY 1969

Cream's 6th single released: 'White Room' backed with 'Those Were The Days'.

Melody Maker prints this news item: 'Eric Clapton and Stevie Winwood may join forces with two members of the late Otis Redding's backing band to record an album.'

Robin Turner (Robert Stigwood spokesman): **It is true that Eric and Stevie have discussed forming a group together and that Eric, while on the Cream's tour of America, did discuss it with Otis Redding's drummer and bass player. But plans are still very fluid at the moment.**

Al Jackon was the drummer who did get to record with Eric, in fact, on his '461 Ocean Boulevard' album in 1974, and Duck Dunn was the bass player who, of course, is now playing and recording in Eric's present band.

FEBRUARY 1969

Eric Clapton: **I don't know whether I'll be doing an album of mine, or an album of mine and Stevie's, or just Stevie's album. It will just have to sort itself out because I can't be bothered making those kind of decisions beforehand.**

MARCH 1969

Eric takes part in a supersession at a TV studio in Staines for a film to be called 'Supershow'.

Eric alongside Roland Kirk, Jon Hiseman, Jack Bruce, Ron Burton, Vernon Martin and Dick Heckstall-Smith perform an instrumental called 'Slate 69' which features a blinding solo by Eric on a Gibson Firebird.

Cream's last LP 'Goodbye' released.

Jackie Lomax LP 'Is This What You Want' is released. Eric appears on 'Sour Milk Sea'.

APRIL 1969

Cream's 7th single released: 'Badge' backed with 'What A Bringdown'.

Ginger Baker joins Eric and Stevie.

GOODBYE

UK Polydor 583053
US Atco SD 7001
Released March 1969

Side One:
1. I'm So Glad
2. Politician
Side Three:
3. Sitting On Top Of The World
4. Badge
5. Doing That Scrapyard Thing
6. What A Bringdown

Right: At the Rolling Stones' Rock And Roll Circus, Wembley, December 10 & 11, 1968. Left to right, back row: John Entwistle, Keith Moon; front row: Yoko Ono, Julian Lennon, John Lennon, Eric Clapton, Brian Jones. (Andre Csillag)

Opposite page: Eric photographed by Lord Snowdon during 1969.

Above: Rehearsing at Eric's home near Guildford with Rick Grech and Steve Winwood for Blind Faith. (Robert Stigwood Organisation)

Eric Clapton: **As far as Stevie Winwood, Ginger Baker and myself are concerned, we are just jamming and we have no definite plans for the future.**

However, by the middle of April, the music press announce that the new band will be giving a free concert in Hyde Park on 7 June followed by a Scandinavian tour and then a US tour opening at the Newport Jazz Festival on 11 July.

They have also been recording quite extensively.

Eric Clapton: **We've been in the studios most of the time and done several songs — one of mine, two by Dylan, one by Buddy Holly and one by Steve. We've got enough to release two albums already.**

MAY 1969

Melody Maker exclusively reveals the name for the new so called supergroup…BLIND FAITH. Bassist Rick Grech, late of Family, joins the other three at Olympic Studios in Barnes to finish recording the band's first LP.

JUNE 1969

Blind Faith's first record release is a studio instrumental issued by Island Records in a limited run of 500 to inform clients of their change of address. Needless to say this is a highly sought after collectors' item, never having been released for public consumption.

7

Hyde Park, London. World première of Blind Faith. They perform a 65 minute set consisting of 'Well All Right', 'Sea Of Joy', 'I'd Rather See You Sleeping On The Ground', 'Under My Thumb', 'Can't Find My Way Home', 'Do What You Like', 'In The Presence Of The Lord', 'Means To An End', and 'Had To Cry Today' as the encore.

Eric plays a Fender Telecaster Custom with a blonde Stratocaster neck for the concert in Hyde Park. The concert was filmed but never released except for one song that was shown on The Bee Gees TV special *Cucumber Castle.*

Rick Grech: **I was nervous at Hyde Park…I think everybody was. We knew the numbers but not to the extent of not having to think about them. I'm sure the majority of the audience expected the band to sound like Cream, and that's not the way it is. Cream were three virtuosos…all improvising. We're not out to outsolo each other.**

12

Short Scandinavian Tour. Martha Velez's album 'Fiends And Angels' is released. Eric plays on 'I'm Gonna Leave You' and 'It Takes A Lot To Laugh, It Takes A Train To Cry'.

JULY 1969
11

Blind Faith's American tour opens at Newport, Rhode Island. The tour turns out to be a disaster for two reasons: because the majority of shows were marred by violence between fans and police, and because fans would give the band standing ovations before even hearing a note. Blind Faith indeed.

They were supported by Free and Delaney and Bonnie on the tour. The set they perform usually runs in the following order: 'Had To Cry Today', 'Can't Find My Way Home', 'I'd Rather See You Sleeping On The Ground', 'Well All Right', 'In The Presence Of The Lord', 'Do What You Like' and 'Sunshine Of Your Love' as the encore with Delaney and Bonnie joining the band onstage. 'Means To An End' and 'Crossroads' were also occasionally included in Blind Faith's set.

12
Madison Square Garden, New York, NY.

16
Spectrum, Philadelphia, Pa.

18
Varsity Stadium, Toronto, Ont.

19
Forum, Montreal, Que.

20
Civic Centre, Baltimore, Md.

23
War Memorial Stadium, Kansas City, Mo.

26
Milwaukee County Stadium, West Allis, Il.

27
International Amphitheatre, Chicago, Il.

AUGUST 1969
Advance orders for the Blind Faith LP reach half a million.

1
Sports Arena, Minneapolis, Mn.

2
Olympia Stadium, Detroit, Mi.

3
Keil Auditorium, St Louis, Mo.

8
PNE Coliseum, Vancouver, BC.

9
Centre Coliseum, Seattle, Wa.

13
Memorial Coliseum, Phoenix, Az.

14
Almeda County Coliseum, Oakland, Ca.

15
Forum, Los Angeles, Ca. 'Blind Faith' LP released. Further press controversy is caused because the cover depicts a nude 11-year-old girl holding a (phallic) silver spaceship.

Left and above: Blind Faith's free concert in Hyde Park, June 7, 1969. (Barry Wentzell & Michael Putland/Retna.

Consequently many record shops refuse to handle the LP in the US and Atco release it in a different sleeve.

***Ahmet Ertegun* (President of Atlantic Records): We haven't withdrawn the other by any means...we have just given people a choice. After all we aren't in the art business.**

***Robert Stigwood*: We just like the design.**

Billy Preston's album 'That's The Way God Planned It' released. Eric plays on 'That's The Way God Planned It (Parts 1 and 2)'.

As the tour progresses Eric spends more and more time with the support band, Delaney and Bonnie, than with the other members of Blind Faith.

1969

Top, far right: Eric with girlfriend Alice Ormsby Gore. (BBC)

Top, near right: Rehearsing at home with Blind Faith. (LFI)

Bottom, far right: With Delaney and Bonnie Bramlett at Heathrow Airport, November 10, 1969. (BBC)

BLIND FAITH

UK Polydor 583059
US Atco SD 33-304
Released August 1969

Side One:
1. Had To Cry Today
2. Can't Find My Way Home
3. Well All Right
4. Presence Of The Lord
Side Two:
5. Sea Of Joy
6. Do What You Like

Delaney Bramlett: **The first time I met Eric was after the first show at New York's Madison Square Garden. We passed the time of day and we got talking. We realised we had both admired the same people, particularly Robert Johnson, and we both had an almost identical collection of records. The only difference was that I had been raised on this music, while Eric had raised himself on it.**

The Los Angeles Forum concert epitomises the violent aspects of the Blind Faith tour. The Forum's house lights are turned on three times during their set to enable police to pursue crowd members. A row of security guards line the front of the stage like an American football team but despite these problems the band play well and the crowd leave happy.

Eric Clapton: **The violence happened everywhere we played. The worst were Los Angeles, New York and Phoenix. When I was with Cream it had not really grown then. Now the kids come to a show with one idea – violence and to heckle the cops.**

By now the rot is setting in, and Eric can feel the end of Blind Faith is in sight.

Eric Clapton: **I don't think the group is going to stay together very long. Stevie's**

going to do something on his own and I will do something on my own.

16
Arena, Santa Barbara, Ca.

20
Male High Stadium, Denver, Co.

22
Salt Palace, Salt Lake City, Ut.

24
HIC Arena, Honolulu, Hi.

26
UCLA Pavley Pavilion, Los Angeles, Ca.

SEPTEMBER 1969
13
Varsity Stadium, Toronto. Eric performs with John Lennon (guitar and vocals), Klaus Voorman (bass), Alan White (drums) and Yoko Ono (vocals). Numbers performed: 'Blue Suede Shoes', 'Money', 'Dizzy Miss Lizzy', 'Yer Blues', 'Cold Turkey', 'Give Peace A Chance', 'Don't Worry Kyoto (Mummy's Only Looking For Her Hand In The Snow)' and 'John, John (Let's Hope For Peace)'. They appear as The Plastic Ono Band.

An amazing concert made all the more remarkable by the fact that this band had not rehearsed other than on the plane over to the concert. The show is recorded and filmed. A video is in circulation amongst collectors.

Eric Clapton: I didn't know anything about it until I got a call from John and I flew out the next morning. It was a great gig and we played well.

On their return, The Plastic Ono Band record some tracks for future release.

Despite this diversion, Blind Faith are technically still together while their members do their own thing. In fact, they never stop doing their own thing and Blind Faith never play again.

OCTOBER 1969

Eric takes part in some abortive studio sessions with Rick Grech, George Harrison, Denny Laine and Trevor Burton. These are for a Rick Grech solo album which remains unreleased.

Plastic Ono Band featuring John Lennon, Yoko Ono, Klaus Voorman, Ringo Starr and Eric Clapton release 'Cold Turkey' backed with 'Don't Worry Kyoto (Mummy's Only Looking For Her Hand In The Snow)' as a single.

Eric has by now decided he'd like to play with Delaney and Bonnie as well as record a solo LP produced by Delaney Bramlett.

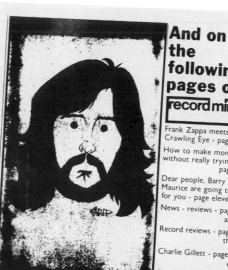

Upset, believed hurt

But Eric Clapton is only a phone call away

BLIND FAITH would appear to be dead although an occasional twitch belies the fact that it is lying down. The intriguing question is why this musical Frankenstein's monster should be mortally wounded after having had a number one album and an apparently successful tour in 'Dollardom'. Clapton, Winwood, Baker and Grech epitomise the musical talent necessary to motivate the Super-group but Faith have stopped motoring and never really made it on to the Highway and so as manager Robert Stigwood reaches for his phone to protest we ask if 'Faith' has been misplaced how did it happen?

The man with some of the answers is musician of the year Eric Clapton whom I spoke to at his home not outside Shere in Surrey where the locals still ironically refer to it as 'The Cream's house'.

After a few minutes conversation with Eric it became quite apparent that to a very large extent the group's present state of immobility and for that matter their musical contraction have been largely caused by the fact they are largely in two minds as to whether they dare chop without a rudder with no one in the Faith wants to be considered an ego-freak.

"There really was no preconceived plan as to how long the group would continue or how permanent it would be," said Eric, as though talking of some lost friend. "The only plan was Steve and I getting together last year and saying we would form a band to record. From that point on everything was coincidental. The fact that we made an album together was a miracle!"

"I thought we played very well on that tour of America although we never really lived up to the expectations of the audience. You can never really live up to that kind of expectations because they

have fantasies about what you will be like — that's why they label you a 'Super-group' before they've even heard you.

But afterwards I realised that we would have been given that reception no matter how we had performed. We could have played 'Knees Up Mother Brown' and they would have flipped out. It was a purely political situation with the cops, the audience and the band.

"Other venues were not so successful and this was partially due to the fact that we had insisted on not stipulating our individual names so that in some areas although they might have come to see Eric Clapton or Ginger Baker or Steve Winwood they had no idea who were the personnel for Blind Faith.

"Another reason was that we were not emotionally what they expected — the expected almost an orgasm — an explosion and they did not get it. There were a lot of compromises to be made in that band and each of us held back.

"I thought originally that Steve and I would be a dominating force behind which Ginger could settle back behind but Steve is a very reticent sort of musician who steps back when he hears someone forcing their way through. I'm a bit like that myself and what happened was that we were all standing back waiting for someone to lead and no one did.

"I'm not sure what is going to happen now, but now I've called the year that American tour and I indication that we are not going to work again or not. If someone rings me and says we have a session I will probably go but I'm not taking it upon myself to get things together.

"There are a few tapes which have been cut lying around the studio but they are just virtually semi-session, and nothing that could be released as an album.

"I intend in future to play with Delaney and Bonnie as they do not have a lead guitarist and my naive self help them in europe where they have not had then album released and are unknown. They come from the South of America — strangely enough there is never any guarantee that a band that good will succeed but they deserve to.

I like most exceptionally talented people Clapton is a sensitive person particularly in those areas which affect his private person.

He admits to being aware of his own huge ego and deliberately suppresses it to the point where he becomes humble. He was delighted to receive an award as 'musician of the year' recently for example but

insists there was no real notification for it because he had not been working in England — his enormous reputation is something which he feels he must fight in a musician.

"Occasionally a critic will say the right thing but generally it's an accident," says Eric. "More often they are saying the wrong thing and disclosing their naivety. Amateur critics are the worst like the DJ I heard the other day on the radio who was putting down The Band.

"Most of them are too concerned with competing with each other and they very seldom assess other than by comparison. They are too fond of comparing the Blind Faith album to say the Humble Pie album and saying one is good and the other is bad. That kind of thing is both irrelevant and unnecessary but most musicians know that."

To some people at least Clapton I fancy or potentially is musically huge as the Faith and if I read the signs currently it is not so much a case of 'missing beloved dead' with Blind Faith but 'upset believed hurt' and like the GPO says 'a phone call brings people closer together' Mr. Winwood.

BY KEITH ALTHAM

RECORD MIRROR, November 5, 1969

And on the following pages of record mirror

Frank Zappa meets the Crawling Eye - page 6

How to make money without really trying - page eight

Dear people, Barry and Maurice are going to write for you - page eleven

News - reviews - page four and five

Record reviews - page thirteen

Charlie Gillett - page eleven

Raggae - page seven

Charts - page fifteen

Polydor telephone message

from AREA CODE 615* time
date 7th Nov
phone 56 546

ASK FOR RUBY

taken by

* Direct dial Nashville, Tennessee.

Eric Clapton: After Blind Faith, Delaney and I then got together and wrote a few songs. I thought it would be a good idea to get them over here and suggested it to the Stigwood Organisation.

NOVEMBER 1969

14

Premiere of 'Supershow' film at the Lyceum, London. Eric takes part in a session for Leon Russell at Olympic Studios in Barnes alongside Klaus Voorman, John Heisman, Carl Radle, Jim Gordon and Chris Stainton.

19

Delaney and Bonnie Bramlett arrive at Eric's country home to rehearse for the upcoming tour together as 'Delaney and Bonnie and Friends with Eric Clapton'.

24

Tour opens in Germany with disastrous receptions.

Bottom left: On tour with Delaney and Bonnie, 1969. (LFI)

1969/70

Delaney Bramlett: We had terrible trouble in Germany. The guy who sold the show put it wrong. People had paid money to see three different groups and then there were only two (Eric with D, B, and F). It was the promoters who were wrong. The kids in Germany had been led to believe Eric Clapton was going to do a single set and not just play with somebody else's band, which of course was incorrect, but the promoters saw it as a quick way to sell tickets.

While in Germany they appear on 'Beat Club' for German television.

DECEMBER 1969

1
British Tour opens at the Royal Albert Hall, London.

2
Colston Hall, Bristol (2 shows 6.15 and 8.45).

3
Town Hall, Birmingham (2 shows 6.15 and 8.45).

4
City Hall, Sheffield (2 shows 6.20 and 8.50).

5
City Hall, Newcastle-upon-Tyne (2 shows 6.15 and 8.45).

6
Empire Theatre, Liverpool (2 shows 6.45 and 9.00). George Harrison sings 'Everybody's Trying To Steal My Baby'.

7
Fairfield Hall, Croydon (2 shows 6.15 and 8.35). This show was recorded for later release as 'On Tour'. The Band consisted of: Delaney Bramlett (rhythm guitar, vocals), Bonnie Bramlett (vocals), Eric Clapton (lead guitar, vocals), Dave Mason (guitar), George Harrison (guitar), Carl Radle (bass), Jim Gordon (drums), Bobby Whitlock (organ, vocals), Jim Price (trumpet, trombone), Bobby Keyes (saxophone), Tex Johnson (conga,

bongo drums), Rita Coolidge (vocals).
George Harrison did not play at the Albert Hall show.

George Harrison: With Delaney and Bonnie there's no expectations because it's really quite anonymous. You just go and do whatever you can do.

Eric Clapton: This is the first tour I've ever been on in my life, and I've been on a good few I can tell you, where everybody has had a good time, and there are a lot of people on this tour.

8
Scandinavia.

9
Scandinavia.

10
Scandinavia.

11
Scandinavia.

12
Falkoner, Copenhagen. Billy Preston joined the 'Friends' for the Scandinavian tour.

15
The Lyceum, London. 'Peace For Christmas' show by the Plastic Ono Band featuring John Lennon, Yoko Ono, Delaney and Bonnie, Eric Clapton, Jim Price, Bobby Keys, Jim

Gordon, Bobby Whitlock, George Harrison, Alan White, Billy Preston, Legs Larry Smith and Keith Moon. This amazing band perform 'Cold Turkey' and 'Don't Worry Kyoto (Mummy's Only Looking For Her Hand In The Snow)'.
The show is recorded and released in 1972 as a free album with John and Yoko's 'Sometime In New York City'.
Plastic Ono Band release their 'Live Peace In Toronto' LP. Eric is on all tracks.
Delaney and Bonnie with Eric Clapton release their single 'Comin' Home' backed with 'Groupie (Superstar)'.
Eric plays on a Vivian Stanshall session.
Eric also adds his guitar talents for a Doris Troy session at Apple Studios in London.

Top and bottom right: With Delaney and Bonnie at the Royal Albert Hall, December 1, 1969. (Chris Walter)

Opposite page
Top: With George Harrison on Delaney and Bonnie tour. (Melody Maker)

Bottom: Backstage at London's Lyceum Ballroom, December 15, 1969. Back row, left to right: Jim Price, Bobby Keyes, Jim Gordon, Klaus Voorman, Bonny and Delaney Bramlett; centre: George Harrison, unknown, Keith Moon, unknown, Eric Barrett, Billy Preston; front: Tony Ashton, John Lennon, Yoko Ono. (Barry Plummer)

JANUARY 1970

Eric enters Village Recorders, Los Angeles, to record his first solo album under the supervision of Delaney Bramlett. Jerry Allison and Sonny Curtis, both from Buddy Holly's Crickets, give their vocal support on this session. The backing musicians are basically 'The Friends' with the addition of John Simon (piano) and Stephen Stills (guitar).

The sessions also produce a track with Atlantic's legendary saxophonist King Curtis called 'Teasin'' as well as two tracks with The Crickets, 'Rocking 50's Rock'n'Roll' and the Buddy Holly classic 'That'll Be The Day'.

FEBRUARY 1970

Short U.S. tour with Delaney and Bonnie including dates at the Fillmore East in New York and Fillmore West in San Francisco.

Vivian Stanshall releases a single 'Labio-Dental Fricative' backed with 'Paper Round'. Both tracks feature some great guitar playing by Eric.

MARCH 1970

Eric returns to England, having completed his solo album and considers several invitations to play sessions.

APRIL, MAY 1970

Eric launches himself into a hectic schedule of session work for Howlin' Wolf, Steve Stills, George Harrison, Ashton, Gardner and Dyke, and Doris Troy.

At the same time a few of 'The Friends' from Delaney and Bonnie become available and come to England to appear on sessions with Eric. They are Jim Gordon, Carl Radle and Bobby Whitlock. It is during sessions for George Harrison that Eric decides to form a group with his old Delaney and Bonnie band friends who are staying with Eric at his house.

Eric Clapton: **I still get a great deal of satisfaction out of playing on someone else's record or singing in with someone else's group. But so far I'm really very keen to do this. (Form Derek and The Dominos.)**

33

1970

Top right: Derek and The Dominoes pictured in Eric's garden. Left to right: Jim Gordon, Carl Radle, Bobby Whitlock and Eric Clapton. (Robert Stigwood Organisation)

Bottom right: (LFI)

Opposite page
Bottom: At London's Lyceum, June 14, 1970. (LFI)

Top left: With Dave Mason at London's Lyceum. (Barry Wentzell)

Bottom left: (SKR)

LIVE CREAM VOL 1

UK Polydor 2382 016
US Atco 33328
Released June 1970

Side One:
1. NSU
2. Sleepy Time Time
3. Lawdy Mama
Side Two:
4. Sweet Wine
5. RYollin' And Tumblin'

JUNE 1970
World première of Eric's new band.

14
Derek and The Dominos perform for Dr. Spock's Civil Liberties Legal Defence Fund at the Lyceum in London. Dave Mason is in the band for this show but he leaves to pursue his solo career in the States.

Eric Clapton: **We are knocked out by the way it went. We only had just over a day's rehearsal and yet it was as if we had been together for months.**

The Dominos continue their session work with George Harrison.
    Release of 'Live Cream' LP.
    Shawn Phillips releases his 'Contribution' LP. Eric plays on 'Man Whole Covered Wagon'.

'Delaney and Bonnie on tour with Eric Clapton' released.
    'Don't You Believe It' single by Jonathan Kelly released. Eric plays on A side.

JULY 1970
Derek and The Dominos record 'Tell The Truth' and 'Roll It Over' augmented by George Harrison during sessions for his upcoming album at EMI's Abbey Road studios. Phil Spector produces the track.
    Eric also plays guitar for a Doctor John session at Trident Studios in London.
    'Teasin'' by King Curtis released as a single. Eric plays on A side.

AUGUST 1970
Derek and The Dominos open their first ever tour with Jim Gordon (drums), Carl Radle (bass), Bobby Whitlock (keyboards and vocals), Eric (guitar and vocals).
    The basic set normally runs as follows: 'Roll It Over', 'Blues Power', 'Have You Ever Loved A Woman', 'Bad Boy', 'Country Life', 'Anyday', 'Bottle Of Red Wine', 'Don't Know Why', 'Tell The Truth'.
    August also sees the release of Eric's first solo album simply called 'Eric Clapton'.

Eric Clapton: The first track on side one will be the instrumental we did, which was 'Just A Good Day' recorded in Los Angeles, when Leon Russell came along. It was just a jam. I'm really pleased with it. It's also matched to another track on the album called 'Blues Power' which is a song that Leon wrote. The words are really applicable to me. And then there's 'Lonesome And A Long Way From Home' which is a song that Delaney Bramlett wrote a long time ago. He was doing it with King Curtis when I arrived in L.A. and Curtis didn't like his voice on it. Curtis doesn't sing much but he's a great singer. So I said I'd like to do a version of it. The next one 'After Midnight' is a song that J.J. Cale wrote. He's one of those people from Tulsa and I think he's an engineer now. He made a record of it and I dug the record a lot so we did our version of that. 'Lovin' You, Lovin' Me' started out as a song that Delaney and Leon wrote for the Blind Faith to do. I liked it very much. I don't know if the others ever heard it. I said I wanted to do it if I ever did a solo album. 'I Don't Know Why' is a ballad, a love song kind of thing. It was an idea that Delaney had when he came to England. 'Get Up And Get Your Man A Bottle Of Red Wine' is a ballad too. We were going to the studio one day in L.A. and we had no songs, nothing at all to do. We were getting panicky on the way and we just thought up the song and did it when we got there. It's just a shuffle. 'I Told You For The Last Time' is a song that Delaney played on acoustic guitar...one of his motel shot numbers I think. We changed that around and arranged it for a big band sort of feel and it came out like a country number really. The last one is called 'She Rides'. That just came from the lyrics of the original song we wrote. But when we went into the studio, the track came off so well that we abandoned the original song and since then I've been trying to think up a set of lyrics to go with the track. That's what has been holding the album up.

1970

All shots from Croydon Fairfield Halls, September 20, 1970. (Barry Plummer)

ERIC CLAPTON

UK Polydor 2383021
UK Atco SD 33329
Released August 1970

Side One:
1. Slunky
2. Bad Boy
3. Told You For The Last Time
4. After Midnight
5. Easy Now
6. Blues Power
Side Two:
7. Bottle Of Red Wine
8. Lovin' You Lovin' Me
9. Lonesome And A Long Way From Home
10. Don't Know Why
11. Let It Rain

The song eventually was titled 'Let It Rain'.

1
Roundhouse, Dagenham.

2
The Place, Hanley, Stoke-on-Trent.

7
Mecca, Newcastle-upon-Tyne.

8
California, Dunstable.

9
Mothers, Birmingham.

11
Marquee, London.

12
Speakeasy, London.

14
Winter Gardens, Malvern.

15
Tofts, Folkestone.

16
Black Prince, Bexley.

18
The Pavilion, Bournemouth.

21
Town Hall, Torquay.

22
Van Dyke Club, Plymouth.

23
Derek and The Dominos fly out to Miami to record at Criteria Studios under the supervision of Tom Dowd.

Tom Dowd: **When I finished doing the 'Layla' album, I walked out of the studio and said, 'That's the best goddamn record I've made in ten years'.**

Thanks to Tom Dowd, Eric is introduced to Duane Allman. Both guitarists had admired each other

from a distance and when they met it was as if they were long lost brothers. Eric immediately asked Duane along to the Criteria sessions.

Duane Allman: **We were playing together and singing a lot acoustically and we got on very well together, like a sort of Laurel and Hardy singing the blues. He came to one of our gigs and that is how I got to know him. He is the only guitarist in London that seems to know what he is doing, and he freaked out when he heard our band. He invited us to go the the studio to play around and that's where it started. I am going to join Eric's band for a few dates towards the end of his tour.**

At the end of the sessions Derek and The Dominos return to the U.K. to continue their tour and play some new numbers which they have just recorded. Their new set usually runs as follows: 'Why Does Love Got To Be So Sad', 'Tell The Truth', 'Blues Power', 'Have You Ever Loved A Woman', 'Keep On Growing', 'Nobody Loves You When You're Down And Out', 'Bottle Of Red Wine', 'Little Wing', 'Roll It Over', 'Bell Bottom Blues' and 'Let It Rain'.
Derek and The Dominos release

their first single 'Tell The Truth' backed with 'Roll It Over'. It is withdrawn at the last minute because of the group's dissatisfaction with the recording.

Group Spokesman: **The group re-recorded 'Tell The Truth' during their studio time in Miami, for inclusion on their new double album. When they compared the two they were so unhappy about the original that they asked Polydor if they could withdraw it. We suggested 'After Midnight' as a single because of pressure from DJs and fans.**

SEPTEMBER 1970
20
Fairfield Hall, Croydon.

21
De Montford Hall, Leicester.

22
Eric flies out to Paris and jams with Buddy Guy and Junior Wells, who are supporting The Rolling Stones at L'Olympia. Eric flies back the next day.

23
Dome, Brighton.

24
Philharmonic Hall, Liverpool.

25
Greens Playhouse, Glasgow.

27
Colston Hall, Bristol.

28
Free Trade Hall, Manchester. Billy Preston releases his 'Encouraging Words' LP. Eric plays on 'Right Now' and 'Encouraging Words'.

OCTOBER 1970
2
College of Technology, Nottingham.

3
Lads Club, Norwich.

4
Coatham Bowl, Redcar.

5
Town Hall, Birmingham. Robert Plant is due to jam, but when he comes on stage one of the road crew ushers him off, not having recognised him.

7
Winter Gardens, Bournemouth.

8
University, Leeds.

9
Penthouse, Scarborough.

11
Lyceum, London. This was the last U.K. show before flying to the U.S. for a long tour.

Chris Charlesworth **(in Melody Maker): When Eric Clapton flew across the Atlantic on Tuesday, his ears were probably still ringing with the applause he collected at London's Lyceum on Sunday. A tighter unit would be hard to find.**

LAYLA AND OTHER ASSORTED LOVE SONGS

UK Polydor 2625005
US Atco SD 2704
Released December 1970

Side One:
1. I Looked Away
2. Bell Bottom Blues
3. Keep On Growing
4. Nobody Loves You When You're Down And Out
Side Two:
5. I Am Yours
6. Anyday
7. Key To The Highway
Side Three:
8. Tell The Truth
9. Why Does Love Got To Be So Bad
10. Have You Ever Loved A Woman
Side Four:
11. Little Wing
12. It's Too Late
13. Layla
14. Thorn Tree In The Garden

Above: Fairfield Halls, Croydon. (Barry Plummer)

Opposite page: Being interviewed by Melody Maker. (Barry Wentzell)

13
Derek and The Dominos fly to New York.

15
Rider College, Trenton, NJ.

16, 17
Electric Factory Theater, Philadelphia, Pa.

21
Lisner Auditorium, Washington, DC.

23, 24
Fillmore East, New York, NY.

29
Kleinhalls Music Hall, Buffalo, NY.

30
Albany State University Gymnasium, Albany, NY.

31
Dome, Virginia Beach, Va. 'After Midnight' backed with 'Easy Now' released as a single.

NOVEMBER 1970

1
Civic Auditorium, Jacksonville, Fl.

5
Johnny Cash TV show, Nashville, Tenn. Eric plays 'It's Too Late' and is joined by Johnny Cash and Carl Perkins for 'Matchbox'.

6
McFarlin Auditorium, Dallas, Tx.

7
Community Centre Theater, San Antonio, Tx.

13
University of Nevada, Reno, Nv.

14
Fairgrounds Coliseum, Salt Lake City, Ut.

17
Memorial Auditorium, Sacramento, Ca.

18, 19
Community Theatre, Berkley, Ca.

20
Civic Auditorium, Santa Monica, Ca.

21
Civic Auditorium, Pasadena, Ca.

22
Community Concourse, San Diego, Ca.

25
Auditorium Theatre, Chicago, Ill.

1970/71

26
Music Hall, Cincinnati, Ohio.

27
Kiel Opera House, St. Louis, Mi.

28
Music Hall, Cleveland, Oh.

29
Painters Mill Music Fair, Owings Mills, Md. George Harrison releases his triple album 'All Things Must Pass'. Eric plays on 'Wah Wah', 'Isn't It A Pity (version one)', 'What Is Life', 'Run Of The Mill', 'Beware Of Darkness', 'Awaiting On You All', 'Plug Me In', 'I Remember Jeep' and 'Thanks For The Pepperoni'.

DECEMBER 1970

1
Curtis Hixon Hall, Tampa, Fl. Duane Allman joins Derek and The Dominos for a couple of shows.

2
War Memorial Auditorium, Syracuse, NY. With Duane Allman.

3
East Town Theater, Detroit, Mi.

4,5
Capitol Theater, Portchester, NY.

6
Suffolk Community College, Selden, NY. Last ever Dominos gig.

7
Eric goes back to Criteria studios to play on and produce a Buddy Guy and Junior Wells session.

JANUARY 1971
Eric attends première of Joe Cocker's 'Mad Dogs And Englishmen' film at the Empire, Leicester Square, London.

FEBRUARY 1971
8
Eric returns to Criteria Studios, Miami, to complete work on the Buddy Guy and Junior Wells album.

Eric Clapton: **What we have left is mainly mixing and a little repolishing.**

The Crickets release their 'Rockin' 50's Rock 'n'Roll' LP. Eric plays on 'Rockin' 50's Rock 'n'Roll' and 'That'll Be The Day'.

APRIL 1971
Jesse Davis releases his solo LP. Eric plays on 'Reno Street Incident', 'Tulsa County', 'Washita Love Child', 'Every Night Is Saturday Night', 'You Bella Donna You', 'Rock And Roll Gypsies', 'Golden Sun Goddess' and 'Crazy Love'.

MAY 1971
Derek and The Dominos break up after a disagreement during the recording of their second album at Olympic Studios in Barnes.
Eric spends the rest of the year at home having slowly become addicted to heroin.

JUNE 1971
'Remember The Yardbirds' LP

Below: Eric deified. This slogan appeared on many walls throughout London during the late sixties. (Roger Perry)

Right: (Barry Wentzell)

released which contains a previously unreleased version of 'I Wish You Would'.

John Mayall releases his 'Back To The Roots' double album. Eric plays on 'Prisons On The Road', 'Accidental Suicide', 'Home Again', 'Looking At Tomorrow', 'Force Of Nature', and 'Goodbye December'.

JULY 1971

Buddy Guy and Junior Wells release 'Play The Blues' LP. Eric plays on 'A Man Of Many Words', 'My Baby She Left Me', 'Come On In This House', 'Have Mercy Baby', 'T. Bone Shuffle', 'A Poor Man's Plea', 'Messin' With The Kid', 'I Don't Know' and 'Bad Bad Whiskey'.

Stephen Stills releases his '2' LP. Eric plays on 'Fishes And Scorpions'.

Bobby Whitlock releases his solo LP. Eric plays on 'Where There's A Will There's A Way', 'A Day Without Jesus', 'Back In My Life Again' and 'The Scenery Has Slowly Changed'.

AUGUST 1971

Howlin' Wolf releases his 'London Sessions' LP. Eric plays on 'Rockin' Daddy', 'I Ain't Superstitious', 'Sittin' On Top Of The World', 'Worried

All shots from the Concert For Bangla Desh, Madison Square Garden, New York, August 1, 1971. (Apple Records)

42

About My Baby', 'What A Woman',
'Poor Boy', 'Built For Comfort',
'Who's Been Talking', 'Little Red
Rooster', 'Do The Do', 'Highway 49',
'Wang Dang Doodle'.

1

Eric comes out of semi-retirement to
help out his friend George Harrison
for a charity concert for the people of
Bangla Desh.

The concert takes place at New
York's Madison Square Garden.
There are two shows, afternoon and
evening. The band for this amazing
show is: George Harrison (guitar,
vocals), Eric Clapton (guitar), Jesse
Davis (guitar), Leon Russell (piano),
Ringo Starr (drums), Klaus
Voormann (bass), Carl Radle (bass),
Jim Keltner (drums), Billy Preston
(organ), Badfinger (backing vocals)
and Don Preston (guitar). Bob Dylan
also appears.

The entire event is filmed and
recorded for later release.

NOVEMBER 1971

Dr. John releases his 'The Sun, Moon
And Herbs' LP. Eric plays on 'Back
John The Conqueror', 'Where Ya At
Mule?', 'Craney Crow', 'Pots On
Fiyo/Who I Got To Fall On', 'Zu Zu
Mandu' and 'Familiar Reality'.

DECEMBER 1971
4

The Rainbow, London. Eric jams
with Leon Russell.

Eric continues his semi-retirement.
His record company release various
compilations to keep his name in the
public eye.

JANUARY 1972

George Harrison's 'The Concert For
Bangla Desh' triple LP released.

JUNE 1972

Cream 'Live – Vol. 2' released.

JULY 1972

Bobby Keys releases his solo LP.
Eric plays on 'Steal From A King',
'Bootleg', 'Command Performance'
and 'Crispy Duck'. 'Layla' backed
with 'Bell Bottom Blues' released as
a single. 'History Of Eric Clapton'
double LP released.

AUGUST 1972

Music press announce that Eric is to
top the bill at the Lincoln Festival
with Stevie Wonder and, according to
Robert Stigwood, the event is to be
recorded. Needless to say, this
never happens.

SEPTEMBER 1972
9

Eric flies out to see The Who in
concert in Paris, after which he
spends time with Keith Richards at
his villa at Villefranche in the South of
France.

John and Yoko release 'Sometime
In New York City'. Eric plays with a
cast of thousands on one side of the
'free' album.

OCTOBER 1972

Eric records with Stevie Wonder at
Air studios in London.

DECEMBER 1972

Bobby Whitlock releases his 'Raw
Velvet' LP. Eric plays on 'Hello L.A.,
Bye Bye Birmingham' and 'The
Dreams Of A Hobo'.

'Duane Allman: An Anthology'
released. This double LP features a
hitherto unreleased track: Duane and
Eric playing 'Mean Old World'. This
LP, an essential purchase for guitar
fans, is a showcase for Duane
Allman's unique talent.

LIVE CREAM VOL 2

UK Polydor 2382 119
US Atco SD 7005
Released July 1972

Side One:
1. Deserted Cities Of The Heart
2. White Room
3. Politician
4. Tales Of Brave Ulysses
Side Two:
5. Sunshine Of Your Love
6. Hideaway

1973

Top right: The comeback concert organised by Pete Townshend at London's Rainbow Theatre, January 13, 1973. (Barry Plummer)

HISTORY OF ERIC CLAPTON

UK Polydor 2659012
US Atco SD 2-803
Released July 1972

Side One:
1. I Ain't Got You
2. Hideaway
3. Tribute To Elmore
4. I Want To Know
5. Sunshine Of Your Love
6. Crossroads
Side Two:
7. Sea Of Joy
8. Only You Know And I Know,
9. I Don't Want To Discuss It
10. Teasin'
11. Blues Power
Side Three:
12. Spoonful
13. Badge
Side Four:
14: Tell The Truth
15. Tell The Truth Jam
16. Layla

JANUARY 1973
13

The Rainbow Theatre, London. Eric performs two shows, one at 6.30 p.m., the other at 8.30 p.m., backed by Pete Townshend, Ronnie Wood, Stevie Winwood, Rebop, Jim Capaldi, Rick Grech and Jimmy Karstein. Support is The Average White Band.

First show set: 'Layla', 'Badge', 'Blues Power', 'Nobody Loves You When You're Down And Out', 'Roll It Over', 'Why Does Love Got To Be So Sad', 'Little Wing', 'Bottle Of Red Wine', 'After Midnight', 'Bell Bottom Blues', 'Presence Of The Lord', 'Tell The Truth', 'Pearly Queen', 'Let It Rain' and 'Crossroads'.

Second show set: 'Layla', 'Badge', 'Blues Power', 'Nobody Loves You When You're Down And Out', 'Roll It Over', 'Why Does Love Got To Be So Sad', 'Little Wing', 'Bottle Of Red Wine', 'Presence Of The Lord', 'Tell The Truth', 'Pearly Queen', 'Key To The Highway', 'Let It Rain', 'Crossroads' and 'Layla (reprise)'.

Pete Townshend: **It really wasn't difficult to get people to help. In fact you might be surprised at a few names I could mention who would have given their right arms to jam in this band.**

Eric Clapton: **I did that very much against my will. It was purely Townshend's idea. I'm indebted to him.**

Eric plays a Fender Stratocaster for the first show and a Gibson Les Paul for the second. The shows are critically acclaimed in the press, but unfortunately when the live album of the event is released it does not evoke the atmosphere of the evening, mainly because it was recorded badly. Eric's comeback was a success and it was a shame that the album did not do justice to the event.

FEBRUARY 1973

Eric and Pete Townshend begin work on unreleased Derek and The Dominos material for possible release.

The rest of the year is spent at home with hardly any contact with the outside world. Although Eric had returned to the stage, he had not yet conquered his heroin addiction. It is later revealed that Eric spent part of the summer working as a farm labourer in Wales.

MARCH 1973

Derek and The Dominos release a live double album 'Live In Concert' recorded at the Fillmore East in New York on 23 October 1970.

APRIL 1973

Derek and The Dominos release a 've single from their double album: 'Why Does Love Got To Be So Sad' backed with 'Presence Of The Lord'.

MAY 1973

'Music From Free Creek' double album released. Eric plays on 'Road Song', 'Getting Back to Molly' and 'No One Knows'.

SEPTEMBER 1973

Eric Clapton's 'Rainbow Concert' LP is released.

Far left: With Ron Wood at the Rainbow. (Barry Plummer)

Near left: With Pete Townshend at the Rainbow. (Barry Wentzell)

Bottom: Flanked by Ron Wood and Pete Townshend at the Rainbow. (Chris Walter)

Eric Clapton's Rainbow Concert with Pete Townshend, Rick Grech, Jim Capaldi, Ronnie Wood, Rebop, Jimmy Karstein, Steve Winwood.

RAINBOW CONCERT

UK RSO 2394116
US RSO 50877
Released September 1973

Side One:
1. **Badge**
2. **Roll It Over**
3. **Presence Of The Lord**
Side Two:
4. **Pearly Queen**
5. **After Midnight**
6. **Little Wing**

45

1974

FEBRUARY 1974

Eric attends Stevie Wonder concert at The Rainbow in London.

APRIL 1974
10

Robert Stigwood throws a party at Soho's China Garden restaurant for Eric to celebrate his return to work.

Eric Clapton: **I don't know why, but I just felt the time was right. I've been talking a lot to Robert about the best way of doing things. So what's happening is I'm going to Miami to record a new album. I'm going to America to form a new band as well. You remember Carl Radle? Well Carl is on bass and he's got a couple of guys together to play keyboards and drums, but I can't really say who they will be yet. It's all just starting to happen. But I want to record again, and I'll also be doing a tour of America and later on some dates in England. There's no name for the band yet, but I don't think it will be called Derek and The Dominos or anything like that. But basically I'm feeling very well. I'm really happy.**

Guests at the party include Elton John, Pete Townshend, Rick Grech, Long John Baldry and Ron Wood.

13

Eric flies to Miami and Criteria Recording Studios where his album will be produced by Tom Dowd.

Top right: Eric announces his comeback plans at the China Garden restaurant, April 10, 1974. (LFI)

Centre and bottom right: In rehearsal, Stockholm, June 20, 1974. (Pictorial Press)

The first few days are difficult with everyone trying to fit in and come up with ideas. However, as the month progressed, so did the music.

MAY 1974

By now Eric has his band together. Carl Radle calls in a couple of his musician friends from Tulsa, Jamie Oldaker (drums) and Dick Sims (keyboards). Yvonne Elliman, wife of Bill Oakes, an RSO executive, is often around the studio, and Eric decides that it would be good to have a female voice in the band to accompany him. Last, but certainly not least, comes George Terry on guitar. He is a local session guitarist that Eric had previously met during the 'Layla' sessions.

They record around 30 tracks. Sessions take place during the night, and during the day they relax in the sunshine at a house at 461 Ocean Boulevard.

JUNE 1974

In preparation for a massive tour, Eric Clapton and His Band, as they are to be known, rehearse in Barbados.

The Eric Clapton Band open with two warm-up shows in Scandinavia.

20

Tivoli Gardens, Stockholm.

21

KB Halle, Copenhagen. Both shows, although a little rough around the edges, are well received.

The band fly off to the States to begin their tour. The set differs every night. They normally open with two or three acoustic numbers before launching into their electric set. The selection comes from the following: 'Smile', 'Easy Now', 'Let It Grow', 'Can't Find My Way Home', which would be acoustic, followed by a selection from: 'I Shot The Sheriff', 'Willie And The Hand Jive', 'Get Ready', 'Presence Of The Lord', 'Steady Rollin' Man', 'Mainline Florida', 'Have You Ever Loved A Woman', 'Blues Power', 'Can't Hold Out', 'Let It Rain', 'Tell The Truth', 'Mean Old World', 'Matchbox', 'Badge', 'Key To The Highway', 'Little Wing', 'Layla', 'Crossroads', 'Little Queenie'.

28
Yale Bowl, Newhaven, Ct.

29
The Spectrum, Philadelphia, Pa.

30
Nassau Coliseum, Uniondale, N.Y.

JULY 1974
2, 3
International Amphitheater, Chicago, Ill.

12

Boston Garden, Boston, Mass.

13

Madison Square Garden, New York, NY. Todd Rundgren jams with Eric on 'Little Queenie'.

14

Capitol Centre, Largo, Md.

19

Long Beach Arena, Long Beach, Ca. John Mayall jams with Eric on a blues shuffle.

20

Long Beach Arena, Long Beach, Ca.

21

Cow Palace, San Francisco, Ca. (2 shows – afternoon and evening).

23

Coliseum, Denver, Co.

24

Coliseum, Denver, Co.

25

Keil Auditorium, St. Louis, Mo.

27

Mississippi Valley Fairgrounds, Davenport, Miss.

28

Memorial Stadium, Memphis, Tenn.

29

Legion Field, Birmingham, Ala.

30

City Park Stadium, New Orleans, Lo. 'I Shot The Sheriff' backed with 'Give Me Strength' released as Eric Clapton Band's first single.

Top left: Copenhagen, June 21, 1974. (Jan Persson)

Bottom: Copenhagen.(Barry Wentzell)

4

Music Park, Columbus, Oh.

5

Three Rivers Stadium, Pittsburgh, Pa. The Band are supporting act on this show and, back at the hotel, Robbie Robertson celebrates his 31st birthday. He is not amused when Eric and Rick Danko attempt to cover him in birthday cake.

6

War Memorial Stadium, Buffalo, N.Y. Eric jams with The Band on 'Stage Fright'. Freddie King jams with Eric on 'Have You Ever Loved A Woman' and 'Hideaway'.

7

Roosevelt Stadium, Jersey City, N.J. Freddie King jams with Eric on 'Have You Ever Loved A Woman'. After the concert Eric's limousine is mobbed by fans as quick getaway tactics break down.

9

The Forum, Montreal, Canada.

10

Civic Centre, Providence, RI.

AUGUST 1974

1

Omni, Atlanta, Ga. Pete Townshend jams with Eric on 'Layla', 'Baby Don't

1974

Top far right: Philadelphia, June 29, 1974. (LFI)

Top near right: Nassau Coliseum, June 30, 1974. (LFI)

Bottom: With rock columnist Lisa Robinson, Nassau Coliseum. (LFI)

461 OCEAN BOULEVARD

UK RSO 2479 118
US RSO SO 4801
Released August 1974

Side One:
1. Motherless Children
2. Give Me Strength
3. Willie And The Hand Jive
4. Get Ready
5. I Shot The Sheriff

Side Two:
6. I Can't Hold Out Much Longer
7. Please Be With Me
8. Let It Grow
9. Steady Rollin' Man
10. Mainline Florida

You Do It', and 'Little Queenie' which also saw Keith Moon join in the proceedings.

2

Coliseum, Greensboro, N. Cal. Pete Townshend jams with Eric on 'Willie And The Hand Jive', 'Get Ready', 'Layla', 'Badge', 'Little Queenie'. Keith Moon jams for the last three numbers.

4

West Palm Beach International Raceway, Palm Beach. Keith Moon sings 'Can't Explain'. Pete Townshend and Joe Walsh also jam with Eric at various points in the concert.

5

Eric and his band go to Criteria Studios in Miami to record with Freddie King before heading off to Dynamic Sounds Studio in Kingston, Jamaica, to record new tracks for their next album.

Marcy Levy, a friend of the Tulsa Rhythm Section, joins the band to add more top harmonies.

Eric releases his new LP '461 Ocean Boulevard'.

Eric Clapton: **This album was very important to me because it was the first thing I'd done in three years and I only had, I think, maybe even only two songs to start it with, and like a snowball it gathered strength as it went along. Also it combined the strength of a new band that I didn't even know until we arrived together in the studio.**

SEPTEMBER 1974

Recording of the new album continues before a short tour of America followed by Japan and Europe. The set changes and Eric and His Band include some newly recorded songs. The set would consist of: 'Smile', 'Let It Grow', 'Better Make It Through Today', 'Can't Find My Way Home', 'Let It Rain', 'Little Wing', 'Singin' The Blues', 'I Shot The Sheriff', 'Tell The Truth', 'The Sky Is Crying', 'Badge', 'Little Rachel', 'Willie And The Hand Jive', 'Get Ready', 'Blues Power', 'Layla', 'All I Have To Do Is Dream', 'Steady Rollin' Man', and 'Little Queenie'.

The set varied every night; some songs were omitted and the running order often changed.

28

Coliseum, Hampton, Va.

29

Nassau Coliseum, Uniondale, N.Y.

OCTOBER 1974
1

The Forum, Montreal, Canada.

2

Maple Leaf Garden, Toronto,
Canada.

6

The Spectrum, Philadelphia, Pa. Eric
and band go to Criteria Studios in

Miami to complete work on their
forthcoming album before embarking
on their first ever tour of Japan.

Howlin' Wolf releases his
'London Revisited' LP. Eric plays on
'Going Down Slow', 'The Killing
Floor' and 'I Want To Have A Word
With You'. (These were outtakes
from the London sessions' LP.)

'Willie And The Hand Jive' backed
with 'Mainline Florida' released as
their second single.

31

Budokan, Tokyo, Japan.

NOVEMBER 1974
1

Budokan, Tokyo.

1974

2
Budokan, Tokyo.

5
Koseinkin Hall, Osaka.

6
Koseinkin Hall, Osaka. After the Japanese tour everyone takes a well deserved break before their European tour.

26
Congress Centrum, Hamburg.

27
Olympia Halle, Munich.

28
Eberthalle, Ludwigshafen.

29
Grugahalle, Essen.

30
Ahoy Hall, Rotterdam. Freddie King releases his 'Burglar' LP. Eric plays on 'Sugar Sweet'.

DECEMBER 1974

1
Palais Des Sports, Anvers.

2
Parc Des Expositions, Paris.

4
Hammersmith Odeon, London.

5
Hammersmith Odeon, London. Ronnie Wood jams with Eric on 'Steady Rollin' Man' and 'Little Queenie'.

There's one in every crowd

Top right: Hammersmith Odeon, December 5, 1974. (Andre Csillag)

Centre right: Hammersmith Odeon. (Barry Wentzell)

Bottom far right and middle: Hammersmith Odeon. (Chris Walter)

Bottom near right: Hammersmith. (LFI)

Left: Madison Square
Garden, New York, July 13,
1974. (Stephen Morley)

1975

Top and centre right: With Pattie at the Leicester Square Theatre, London, for the premiere of The Who's 'Tommy' movie, March 27, 1975. (BBC)

Bottom right: With Pattie at Heathrow Airport, February 28, 1975. (BBC)

THERE'S ONE IN EVERY CROWD

UK RSO 2479132
US RSO SO 4806
Released April 1975

Side One:
1. We've Been Told (Jesus Coming Soon)
2. Swing Low Sweet Chariot
3. Little Rachel
4. Don't Blame Me
5. The Sky Is Crying
Side Two:
6. Singin' The Blues
7. Better Make It Through Today
8. Pretty Blue Eyes
9. High
10. Opposites

MARCH 1975

Eric and girlfriend Pattie Harrison attend London première of 'Tommy' at the Leicester Square Theatre. Eric appears as the Preacher performing 'Eyesight To The Blind'.

APRIL 1975

Eric is advised to become a tax exile and his new base is a luxury villa in the Bahamas. He is allowed sixty days a year in England provided he doesn't play live.

The set for this tour varies each night and is taken from the following: 'Badge', 'Steady Rollin' Man', 'Key To The Highway', 'Milk Cow Blues', 'Can't Find My Way Home', 'Teach Me To Be Your Woman', 'Nobody Loves You When You're Down And Out', 'I Shot The Sheriff', 'Layla', 'Little Wing', 'Tell The Truth', 'Let It Grow'.

7
Hic Arena, Honolulu, Hawaii.

8
Hic Arena, Honolulu, Hawaii.

10
Auckland, New Zealand. Eric plays to 18,000 people.

14
Festival Hall, Brisbane, Australia.

15
Festival Hall, Melbourne, Australia.

16
Festival Theatre, Adelaide, Australia.

18
Concert Hall, Perth, Australia.

20
Opera House, Sydney, Australia.

21
Opera House, Sydney, Australia.

22
Theatre Centre, Canberra, Australia. Eric returns home to England for a week, only to have a close shave with a juggernaut in which his Ferrari is very badly damaged. A picture of the car appears on the inside sleeve of the 'Slowhand' album.

Eric releases his new album 'There's One In Every Crowd'.

Eric Clapton: **It's the kind of record that if you didn't like it after maybe the third or fourth time, you wouldn't play it again. But if you did like it and you carried on listening to it, you'd hear things that were really fine, just little things in the background, little touches.**

'Swing Low Sweet Chariot' backed with 'Pretty Blue Eyes' released as their third single.

MAY 1975

Eric spends most of May resting before rehearsing for a U.S. tour.

JUNE 1975

Start of massive U.S. tour which will
last till 30 August with a break in the
middle.

Prime Cuts (10″ maxi sampler)
released. A live unreleased version
of Eric performing 'Smile' is featured.

The set again varies every night
and is taken from the following:
'Layla', 'Bell Bottom Blues', 'Key To
The Highway', 'Mainline Florida',
'Keep On Growing', 'Can't Find My
Way Home', 'Carnival', 'Stormy
Monday', 'Little Wing', 'Tell The
Truth', 'Why Does Love Got To Be
So Sad', 'Teach Me To Be Your
Woman', 'Badge', 'Let It Rain',
'Blues Power', 'Knockin' On
Heaven's Door', 'Further On Up The
Road' and 'Eyesight To The Blind'
(Carlos Santana jammed on this
number most nights during the first
half of the tour).

16

Tampa Stadium, Tampa, Fl.

22

Jams with The Rolling Stones at
Madison Square Garden on
'Sympathy For The Devil'.

1975

23
Convention Center, Niagara Falls.

24
Springfield, Mass.

25
Civic Center, Providence, RI. Eric performs 'Sunshine Of Your Love' for the first time since Cream disbanded.

28
Nassau Coliseum, Uniondale, N.Y. Carlos Santana, John McLaughlin and Alphonse Mouzon jam with Eric on 'Eyesight To The Blind'. 'Further On Up The Road' from the LP 'EC Was Here' is recorded at this show.

JULY 1975
1
Olympia Stadium, Detroit, Mich.

4
Richfield Coliseum, Cleveland, Ohio.

8
Dane County Coliseum, Madison, Wi. Eric performs 'Sunshine Of Your Love' again.

11
Keil Auditorium, St. Louis, Mo. 'Tommy' soundtrack LP released. Eric plays on 'Eyesight To The Blind' and 'Sally Simpson'.

28
Eric plays on a Bob Dylan session at Columbia Studios in New York.

AUGUST 1975
9
University, Stanford, Ct.

11
Salt Palace, Salt Lake City, Ut.

12
Coliseum, Denver, Co.

14
The Forum, Los Angeles, Ca. Keith Moon jams alongside Carlos Santana and Joe Cocker on tambourine.

15
Swing auditorium, San Bernadino, Ca. Jerry McGee jams with Eric on 'Further On Up The Road' and 'Stormy Monday'.

16
Sports Arena, San Diego, Ca.

17
ASU Stadium, Tempe, Ar.

18
Community Center, Tucson, Ar.

20
Sam Houston Coliseum, Houston, Tx.

Club of Ireland at Straffan House, home of Kevin McClory, the film producer, for a charity show alongside the likes of Shirley MacLaine, Judy Geeson, Sean Connery and Burgess Meredith, with music supplied by The Chieftains. A 37 minute film of the event is released and is called *Circasia*.

Eric stays in Ireland for a break in County Kildare.

Eric releases his live album 'EC Was Here'.

Eric Clapton: **There was a long battle about this album and I refused to let it go out until I heard...I think it was 'Have You Ever Loved A Woman' and it was played to me by Tom Dowd in the studio in Criteria, and he just said, 'Listen to this' and the rest of it was built round that for me. He convinced me with that one track that it was worth doing a live album and he had complete control over what went on there.**

Towards the end of September Eric heads off to New York for some recording before starting a Japanese tour.

OCTOBER 1975
The Japanese set is virtually the same as U.S.A '75.

22, 23
Koseinkin Hall, Osaka.

24
Kyoto Kaikan, Kyoto.

26
Sunpan Kaikan, Shizuoka.

NOVEMBER 1975
1, 2
Budokan, Tokyo. Dr. John releases his 'Hollywood Be Thy Name' LP. Eric plays congas on 'Reggae Doctor'.

EC WAS HERE

UK RSO 2394160
US RSO SO 4809
Released August 1975

Side One:
1. Have You Ever Loved A Woman
2. Presence Of The Lord
3. Drifting Blues
Side Two:
4. Can't Find My Way Home
5. Rambling On My Mind
6. Further On Up The Road

21
Tarrant County Convention Center, Fort Worth, Tx.

22
Hirsch Coliseum, Shreveport, Lo.

23
Myria, Oklahoma, Ok.

27
Market Sq. Arena, Indianapolis, In.

28
Charleston, S.Ca.

29
Coliseum, Greensboro, S.Ca.

30
The Scope, Norfolk, Va. Poco jam with Eric on 'Let It Rain'.

Eric Clapton: **You won't catch me saying this is my best band. The last time I said that The Dominos broke up a month later. But I'd go see us.**

'Knockin' On Heaven's Door' backed with 'Someone Like You' released as a single by Eric.

'Knockin' On Heaven's Door' backed with 'Plum' released by Arthur Louis. Eric plays on both tracks.

Arthur Louis releases his 'First Album' in Japan only. Eric plays on 'Knockin' On Heaven's Door', 'Plum', 'The Dealer', 'Still It Feels Good', 'Come On And Love Me', 'Train 444', 'Go And Make It Happen'.

SEPTEMBER 1975
Eric returns to England for a short vacation in the U.K.

11
Hammersmith Odeon, London. Santana play the Odeon and bring on Eric for the encore. Unfortunately, he couldn't even jam as he was still a tax exile.

14
Eric appears as a clown for the Central Remedial Clinic and Variety

1976

NO REASON TO CRY

UK RSO 2394160
US RSO 1-3004
Released August 1976

Side One:
1. Beautiful Thing
2. Carnival
3. Sign Language
4. County Jail Blues
5. All Our Past Times
Side Two:
6. Hello Old Friend
7. Double Trouble
8. Innocent Times
9. Hungry
10. Black Summer

Centre right: Hemel
Hempstead Pavilion, July 29,
1976. (Andre Csillag)

JANUARY 1976
Bob Dylan releases his 'Desire' album. Eric plays on 'Romance In Durango'.

FEBRUARY, MARCH, APRIL 1976
The early part of the year is spent at The Band's Shangri-La Studio for the recording of 'No Reason To Cry'. Many guests drop by the studio for various jams and guest spots: Bob Dylan, Ronnie Wood, Robbie Robertson (who contributes some stunning lead guitar work on the Dylan track 'Sign Language'), Rick Danko, Levon Helm, Garth Hudson and Richard Manuel to name but a few.

Eric Clapton: I think my best stuff has been done in American studios. Shangri-La was the finest studio of all to work in. We cut something like twenty five tracks in three weeks out of nowhere, out of the blue. It was just like falling rain, and the outtakes...whoever's got them is sitting on a mint, because they're beautiful. Some of the best stuff didn't get on the album...like instrumentals.

I had a magnificent birthday party right in the middle of the sessions and we decided to record everything and everybody that came into the studio. There's Billy (Preston) singing a couple of Ray Charles songs with The Band backing him along with Jesse Ed Davis, me, Robbie (Robertson) and Woody (Ron Wood) on guitars. Bob (Dylan) showed up about eight o'clock in the morning and it went on from there.

During this period Eric also jammed with The Crusaders at The Roxy in Los Angeles along with Stevie Wonder, Elton John and Rick Danko. He also took part in a session for a Van Morrison album which remains unreleased.

MAY 1976
15
Granby Halls, Leicester. Jams with The Rolling Stones on 'Brown Sugar" and 'Key To The Highway'.

JUNE 1976
Joe Cocker releases his 'Stingray' LP. Eric plays on 'Worrier'.

JULY 1976
29
British Tour opens at the Pavilion, Hemel Hempstead. The show opens with two acoustic numbers 'Hello Old Friend' and 'All Our Past Times'. The remainder of the set varies each night but would be taken from the following: 'I Shot The Sheriff', 'Nobody Loves You When You're Down And Out', 'Can't Find My Way Home', 'Tell The Truth', 'Kansas City', 'Innocent Times', 'Stormy Monday', 'Goin' Down Slow', 'Double Trouble', 'Blues Power', 'Layla', 'Key To The Highway', 'Knocking On Heaven's Door' and 'Further On Up The Road'.

Right: All shots from Crystal
Palace Bowl concert,
London, July 31, 1976.
(Barry Plummer)

Top near left: Crystal Palace.
(Camera Press)

LETTERS

dear everybody....

i openly apologise to all the foreiguers in Brum.... its just that (as usual) i'd had a few before i went on, and one foreigner had pinched my missuss' bum and proceeded to lose my bottle, well, you know the rest, anyway, im off up the pub, and i dont live in america, and i think i think that enoch is the only politician mad enough to run this country..... yours humbly eccentricly

E.C.

P.S. and if you dont this print you will all be arrested P.C.

The band consists of Eric Clapton (guitar, vocals), George Terry (guitar, vocals), Carl Radle (bass), Dick Sims (keyboards), Jamie Oldaker (drums), Sergio Pastora Rodriguez (percussion), Marcy Levy (vocals), Yvonne Elliman (vocals).

31

Crystal Palace Bowl, London. This was the ninth Garden Party at the Bowl and support artists were Freddie King, The Jess Roden Band, Barbara Dixon, Dick And The Firemen and The Chieftains.
Larry Coryell jams with Eric on 'Going Down Slow' and 'Stormy Monday' as well as the encore of 'Further On Up The Road' which also saw Freddie King and Ronnie Wood join them.

AUGUST 1976

1
Gaumont, Southampton.

2
Town Hall, Southampton.

3
ABC Theatre, Plymouth.

5
Odeon, Birmingham. Van Morrison joins Eric for 'Kansas City' and a few blues numbers. This is the gig where Eric makes his controversial political speech, apparently in support of Enoch Powell.

Eric Clapton: **I just don't know what came over me that night. It must have been something that happened in the day but it came out in this garbled thing. I'm glad you printed the letter though.**

The letter Eric refers to is the one he sent to *Sounds* (issue September 11 1976) after hostile press over-reaction. In it he gave the reasons for his behaviour.

6
Belle Vue King's Hall, Manchester. Van Morrison again joins Eric for 'Kansas City' and a few blues numbers.

7
University, Lancaster.

9, 10
Apollo, Glasgow.

12
City Hall, Newcastle-upon-Tyne.

13
Spa Pavilion, Bridlington.

15
ABC Theatre, Blackpool. Eric and band sing 'Happy Birthday' to Roger Forrester, his manager, during their set.

17
Warner Holiday Camp, Hayling Island. Eric plays to impartial

1976

holidaymakers numbering under 1000. No members of the public are allowed in.

Promoter Harvey Goldsmith: **I haven't heard him play like this the whole tour.**

Eric Clapton: **I'm always more comfortable in situations like that. The pressures are off and I feel comfortable because there is no one to prove myself to.**

SEPTEMBER 1976

7

Eric and Pattie Harrison attend Buddy Holly's 40th birthday anniversary party in the company of Paul and Linda McCartney, Elton John, Phil Manzanera, Andy Mackay, Stephen Bishop, Steve Harley and Eric Stewart to name but a few. Norman Petty, Buddy Holly's producer and co-writer, is guest of honour.

Eric writes 'Wonderful Tonight' after the party.

Eric Clapton: **The songs you write very quickly are always the best...the ones that are written in the space of a day. It was just about taking the old woman out and getting too sloshed to drive home.**

17

Eric and Pattie attend Croydon's Fairfield Hall for the start of Don Williams British tour.

Eric invites everyone back to his house for a jam session which lasts well into the early hours.

18

Eric joins Don Williams on stage at Hammersmith Odeon in London to play some of the finest dobro you're likely to hear. Eric also introduces Pete Townshend and Ronnie Lane to Williams backstage.

Don Williams: **He's an incredible picker. Eric plays a lot of rhythms and stuff that are very close to the way I feel and some of the songs he's written are just...really fine. He's phenomenal.**

Ringo Starr releases his 'Rotogravure' LP. Eric wrote and plays on 'This Be Called A Song'.

Top right: With Pattie designing album covers. (Graham Wiltshire)

Bottom right: Crystal Palace. (Andre Csillag)

58

Top and bottom left: Crystal Palace. (Relay Photos)

NOVEMBER 1976

5

Short U.S. tour opens at the Bayfront Center in St. Petersburg, Florida. Same band as British tour.

Shows open with two acoustic numbers, 'Hello Old Friend' and 'Sign Language'. The remainder of the set varies each night but is taken from the following: 'Tell The Truth', 'Double Trouble', 'Knocking On Heaven's Door', 'Blues Power', 'Can't Find My Way Home', 'Key To The Highway', 'I Shot The Sheriff', 'One Night', 'Layla', 'Further On Up The Road', 'Badge' and 'Have You Ever Loved A Woman'.

6

Sportatorium, Miami, Fl.

7

Coliseum, Jacksonville, Fl.

9

Omni, Atlanta, Ga.

10

Municipal Auditorium, Mobile, Al.

11

LSU Assembly Center, Baton Rouge, Lo.

13

Hofhienz Pavilion, Houston, Tx.

14

Eric joins Texas Blues Jam playing alongside Bugs Henderson, Freddie King, Bobby Chitwood and Ron Thompson.

15

Memorial Auditorium, Dallas, Tx. Freddie King joins Eric on 'Further

On Up The Road'. The majority of the show is broadcast at a later date by the King Biscuit Boy Flower Hour program.

16

Myriad, Oklahoma City, Ok.

20

Sports Arena, San Diego, Ca.

22

The Forum, Los Angeles, Ca.

26

Winterland, San Francisco, Ca. Eric joins a cast of thousands for The Band's farewell concert. Eric plays 'Further On Up The Road' and 'All Our Pastimes' backed by The Band. He returns to join Van Morrison, Ron Wood, Bob Dylan, Neil Young, Joni Mitchell, Ronnie Hawkins, Dr. John,

1976/77

Neil Diamond, Paul Butterfield, Bobby Charles, Ringo Starr and, of course, The Band, for a rendition of 'I Shall Be Released'. Finally, Eric, along with Steve Stills, Carl Radle, Ronnie Wood, Neil Young, Robbie Robertson, Levon Helm, Ringo Starr, Paul Butterfield and Dr. John return to the stage for a couple of instrumental jams.

A large amount of the concert is released both on album and video as 'The Last Waltz'. The highlight is Muddy Waters' amazing version of 'Mannish Boy'.

Eric also finds time to jam with Freddie King at the Starwood in Los Angeles along with Bonnie Bramlett.

DECEMBER 1976

Stephen Bishop releases his first solo album 'Careless'. Eric plays on 'Sinking In An Ocean Of Tears' and 'Save It For A Rainy Day.'

FEBRUARY 1977
14

Eric plays an unpublicised St. Valentine's Day dance at Cranleigh Village Hall in Surrey.

The concert posters advertise the group as Eddie and The Earth Tremors, although it is common knowledge locally who is appearing. The evening is arranged by the local Round Table charity. As Eric takes a keen interest in local affairs, he is only too happy to play for nothing as long as his name is not mentioned. As a result Cranleigh Cottage Hospital benefits by £1000.

Top right: With Pattie and Stephen Bishop, December, 1976. (Alan Messer)

Centre and bottom right: At Cranleigh Village Hall, February 14, 1977. (Barry Plummer)

Near right: Robbie Roberston and Rick Danko of The Band with Ronnie Hawkins at the Last Waltz concert, San Francisco, November 26, 1976. (United Artists)

Left: Hammersmith Odeon,
April 27, 1977. (Barry
Plummer and Paul Cox)

1977

Top right: Hammersmith Odeon, April 27, 1977. (Barry Plummer)

Backed by Ronnie Lane (guitar and vocals), Bruce Rowland (drums), Charlie Hart (accordion, violin, keyboards) and Brian Belshaw (bass) this one off band performs such songs as 'How Come', 'Willie And The Hand Jive', 'Oo La La', 'Goodnight Irene' and 'Alberta, Alberta'. A good time is had by all.

Kinky Friedman releases his 'Lasso From El Passo' LP. Eric plays on 'Kinky' and 'Ol' Ben Lucas'.

February also sees the release of 'Carnival' backed with 'Hungry' as a single.

APRIL 1977
20
British tour opens at the De Montfort Hall, Leicester. Shows open with acoustic versions of 'Hello Old Friend', 'Sign Language' and 'Alberta, Alberta' followed by an electric set which is taken from the following: 'Tell The Truth', 'Knocking On Heaven's Door', 'Steady Rollin' Man', 'Can't Find My Way Home', 'Further On Up The Road', 'Stormy Monday', 'Badge', 'Nobody Loves You When You're Down And Out', 'I Shot The Sheriff', 'Layla', 'Key To The Highway',

'Willie And The Hand Jive' and 'Crossroads'.

The band is the same as the 1976 line up.

21
Free Trade Hall, Manchester.

22
Stoke On Trent.

23
Apollo Theatre, Glasgow.

24
City Hall, Newcastle-upon-Tyne.

26
BBC TV Theatre, Shepherds Bush, London.

27
Hammersmith Odeon, London.

28
Hammersmith Odeon, London. Ronnie Lane and Patti join Eric for 'Willie And The Hand Jive'. Rose

Clapp also runs across the stage to give Eric a huge hug.

29
The Rainbow Theatre, London. Pete Townshend jams with Eric on 'Layla' and 'Crossroads'.

MAY 1977
Eric and his band enter Olympic Studios in Barnes for the recording of 'Slowhand' with Glyn Johns producing. Mel Collins on sax guests on 'The Core'.

Eric Clapton: **'Slowhand' for me is a very nervous sung album, especially after 'No Reason To Cry'. Maybe it was because of the lack of material we had when we went in to cut it or the difference in surroundings. Anyway, for me the best track has got to be 'Wonderful Tonight' because the song is nice. It was written about my sweetheart, and whether or not it was recorded well or I played it well doesn't make any difference, because the song is still nice.**

Corky Laing releases his LP 'Makin' It On The Street'. Eric plays on 'On My Way'.

Roger Daltrey releases his 'One Of The Boys' LP. Eric is credited.

JUNE 1977

4
National Stadium, Dublin.

6
National Stadium, Dublin.

9
Falconer Theatre, Copenhagen.

10
Stadthalle, Bremen.

11
Groenoordhal, Leiden.

13
Forest National, Brussels.

14
Le Pavilion, Paris. Ringo Starr on tambourine joins Eric for 'Badge'.

16
Eisstadion, Wetzikon.

20
Olympia Halle, Munich. For this European tour Eric hires the dining car from the Orient Express, one elegant day coach and one sleeper car from Denmark.

Eric Clapton: It is the only way to travel. I'm amazed how well it's worked. I really thought that we'd wake up one morning and find ourselves hundreds of miles away on the wrong side of Europe. Now I don't want to travel any other way.

JULY 1977

Eric and Patti take a short holiday on board Robert Stigwood's yacht 'The Welsh Liberty' which takes them from Nice to Ibiza for a short tour.

AUGUST 1977

5
The Bull Ring, Ibiza.

11
Nouveau Pabellon Club, Barcelona.

Eric Clapton: In Ibiza, when you walked into the dressing room, there was the operating table with blood gutters down the side of it for the matadors, when they get patched up. It was all a bit grim. I thought it was going to be a lovely old building like a rodeo place and it turned out to be a concrete monstrosity in the middle of nowhere.

SEPTEMBER 1977

Start of short Japanese tour. The band is basically the same as the European tour except that Sergio Pastora and Yvonne Elliman had now left.

The set is taken from the following: 'The Core', 'Badge', 'Double Trouble', 'Knockin' On Heaven's Door', 'Bottle Of Red Wine', 'Nobody Loves You When You're Down And Out', 'Alberta, Alberta', 'We're All The Way', 'Sign Language', 'Tell The Truth', 'Stormy Monday', 'Layla' and 'Key To The Highway'.

26
Festival Hall, Osaka.

27
Japan.

28
Japan.

29
Japan.

30
Japan. Pete Townshend and Ronnie Lane release 'Rough Mix' LP. Eric

Bottom left: Hammersmith Odeon, April 28, 1977. (Relay Photos)

1977/78

plays on 'Rough Mix', 'Annie', 'April Fool' and 'Till The Rivers All Run Dry'.

OCTOBER 1977

1
Festival Hall, Osaka.

2
Japan.

3
Japan.

Top far right: Jamie Oldaker. (Michael Putland)

Top near right: Pattie behind the camera. (Michael Putland)

Centre far right: Marcy Levy. (Michael Putland)

Centre near right: Pattie adjusts Eric's sartorial image. (Michael Putland)

Below centre: George Terry, Dick Simons with their boss. (Michael Putland)

Bottom: (Michael Putland)

Opposite page: USA, 1978. (Michael Putland)

SLOWHAND

SLOWHAND

UK RSO 2479201
US RSO RS 1-3030
Released November 1977

Side One:
1. Cocaine
2. Wonderful Tonight
3. Lay Down Sally
4. We're All The Way

Side Two:
5. The Core
6. May You Never
7. Mean Old Frisco
8. Peaches And Diesel

4
Japan.

5
Japan.

6
Budokan, Tokyo.

7
Budokan, Tokyo. After Japan Eric heads to Hawaii for a few dates in Honolulu.

Freddie King album '1934-1976' is released. Eric plays on 'Sugar Sweet', 'TV Mama', 'Gambling Woman Blues' and 'Further On Up The Road'.

NOVEMBER 1977

'Lay Down Sally' backed with 'Cocaine' is released as a single.

Eric releases his new LP titled 'Slowhand'.

JANUARY 1978

Rick Danko releases his solo LP. Eric plays on 'New Mexico'.

FEBRUARY 1978

1
U.S. tour opens at the PNE Coliseum, Vancouver, Canada. As always the set would vary from night to night but would be taken from the following: 'Peaches And Diesel', 'Wonderful Tonight', 'Lay Down Sally', 'Next Time You See Her', 'The Core', 'All The Way', 'Rodeo Man', 'Fools Paradise', 'Cocaine', 'Badge', 'Let It Rain', 'Knockin' On Heaven's Door', 'Key To The Highway', 'Going Down Slow', 'Layla', 'Bottle Of Red Wine', 'You'll Never Walk Alone'.

The band consists of Eric Clapton (guitar, vocals), George Terry (guitar, vocals), Carl Radle (bass), Dick Sims (keyboards), Jamie Oldaker (drums), Marcy Levy (vocals).

3
Exhibition Coliseum, Edmonton, Canada.

1978

Top right: US tour, 1978.
(Michael Putland)

Bottom far right:
Hammersmith Odeon,
December 1978. (Barry
Plummer)

Bottom near right: US tour,
1978. (Neal Preston)

5
Paramount Theater, Seattle, Wash.

6
WSU Coliseum, Pullman, Wash.

8
Paramount Theater, Portland, Ore.

10
Coliseum, Oakland, Ca.

11, 12
Civic Auditorium, Santa Monica, Ca.

13
Aladdin Theater, Las Vegas, Ne.

15
McNichols Arena, Denver, Co.

18
Metropolitan Center, Minneapolis,
Minn.

19
University of Iowa Hilton Coliseum,
Ames, Iowa.

20
Convention Centre, Kansas City,
Ka.

21
Keil Auditorium, St. Louis, Mo.

23
Stadium, Chicago, Ill.

24
Gardens, Louisville, Ky.

26
Civic Center Arena, Huntington, Ind.

28
Municipal Auditorium, Nashville,
Tenn. Don Williams opens this show
for Eric with a great 30 minute set
including such songs as 'I Recall A
Gypsy Woman' and 'Shelter Of Your
Eyes'.

Don Williams: **It was tough, but I expected it to be an uphill fight, Eric and I really want to work together more because we appreciate each other's music so much. Hopefully we'll get to try it out some other places and maybe approach it a little differently.**

MARCH 1978

'Wonderful Tonight' backed with 'Peaches And Diesel' released as a single.

1

Mid-South Coliseum, Memphis, Tenn.

2

Boutwell Auditorium, Birmingham, Al.

3

Eric returns to the U.K. for a breather from the tour, on which he has decided to play small venues.

Eric Clapton: **It's a deliberate move. I don't play the huge stadiums now, because I want to get closer to the audiences. Until now they've never seen me at my best in America. I can't wait to get back there.**

11

Attends West Bromwich Albion v. Nottingham Forest match. W.B.A. – whom Eric supports – win.

17

Returns to U.S.A. for continuation of tour.

19

Jai-Alai Frontun, Miami, Fla.

20

Civic Center Coliseum, Lakeland, Fla.

21

Civic Center, Savannah, Ga.

22

Coliseum, Macon, Ga.

Top left: Eric and Don Williams, 1978. (Richard Young)

Bottom left: With Bob Dylan, Blackbushe, July 15, 1978.

24

Memorial Coliseum, Charlotte, Va.

25

Carolina Coliseum, Columbia, S.Cal.

26

Von Braun Civic Center, Huntsville, Ala. King Biscuit Flower Hour broadcast 90 minutes of Eric's Santa Monica show from 11.2.78.

28

Cobo Hall, Detroit, Mich.

29

Convention Center, Cleveland, Ohio.

31

Civic Center Arena, Baltimore, Md.

APRIL 1978

1

The Spectrum, Philadelphia, Pa.

2, 3

Radio City Music Hall, New York, N.Y.

5

Civic Center, Springfield, Mass.

7

The Forum, Montreal, Canada.

9

Maple Leaf Gardens, Toronto, Canada.

19

Pinewood Studios. Eric takes part in

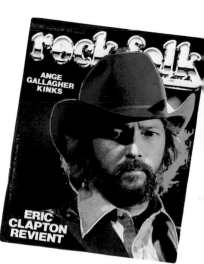

1978

Alexis Korner's 50th birthday party celebrations. This show will later be available on video and record.

Eric and band take a well deserved holiday and prepare themselves for a series of festival appearances as support for Bob Dylan.

I Jah Man releases his 'Haile I Hymn' LP. Eric was at the sessions along with Stevie Winwood.

The Band's 'Last Waltz' LP is released. Eric plays on 'Further On Up The Road' and 'I Shall Be Released'.

JUNE 1978
23

Feijenoord Stadium, Rotterdam. This is the first of three dates supporting Bob Dylan.

June also sees the release of the 'White Mansions' LP. Eric plays on 'White Trash' and 'Kentucky Racehorse'.

JULY 1978
1

Zeppelinfield, Nuremburg. After his own set Eric joins Bob Dylan for 'I'll Be Your Baby Tonight', and 'The Times They Are A-Changin''.

7, 8

National Stadium, Dublin. These two dates are used as a warm up for their forthcoming show at the huge Blackbushe Festival.

15

Blackbushe Aerodrome, Hampshire. 200,000 people attend the last date of Bob Dylan's European tour. Support acts are Merger, Lake, Graham Parker, Eric Clapton and Joan Armatrading.

£1,270,000 is the staggering amount of gate money, £350,000 going to Bob Dylan.

Eric joins Dylan for a rousing guitar solo on 'Forever Young'.

Top right: With Dylan at Blackbushe. (Barry Plummer)

Centre right: Blackbushe. (Simon Fowler)

AUGUST, SEPTEMBER 1978

Eric and band enter Olympic Studios in Barnes to record 'Backless' with

Glyn Johns producing.

Bob Dylan gives Eric two unreleased songs to record, 'Walk Out In The Rain' and 'If I Don't Be There By Morning'.

Benny Gallagher and Graham Lyle guest on 'Golden Ring'.

Eric Clapton: **The title came from the Dylan gig we did at Blackbushe, where it became very apparent that he knew exactly what was going on around him all the time. So it's a tribute to Bob, really. I mean...if you were backstage, he expected you to be putting as much into it as he was. You couldn't just stand there and be one of the roadies, you had to actually focus all your attention on him, and if you didn't, he knew it, and he'd turn around and he'd look at you and you'd get daggers**

The best things that happened on 'Backless' were the things that happened at the time. I got away with one song, 'Golden Ring', which I think is the strongest song on the album, because I wrote it because I was fed up with the general sort of apathy of everyone involved, and I just thought, "Well, I'll take a song in there and whether they like it or not, we'll do it – they'll learn it and record it and we'll put it on the record, and that's that'. And that kind of conviction carried the thing through.

'Promises' backed with 'Watch Out For Lucy' released as a single.

OCTOBER 1978

Eric and band, which now consists only of Jamie Oldaker, Carl Radle and Dick Sims, rehearse for the

forthcoming European tour.

As usual the sets vary each night and are to be taken from the following: 'Golden Ring', 'Someone Like You' (B-side of 'Knockin' On Heaven's Door'), 'Loving You', 'Layla', 'Worried Life Blues', 'Tulsa Time', 'Early In The Morning', 'I'll Make Love To You Anytime', 'Double Trouble', 'Badge', 'Wonderful Tonight', 'If I Don't Be There', 'Key To The Highway', 'Cocaine', 'Crossroads' and 'Further On Up The Road'.

Muddy Waters is the support act for the tour and he would often jam during Eric's encore.

NOVEMBER 1978

5
Pabellon Deportivo Del Real Madrid, Madrid.

6
Club Juventus, Barcelona.

8
Palais Des Sports, Lyon.

10
Saarlandhalle, Saarbrucken.

11
Festhalle, Frankfurt.

12
Olympia Halle, Munich.

14
Phillipshalle, Dusseldorf.

15, 16
Congresscentrum, Hamburg.

18
Le Pavilion, Paris.

Top and centre left: UK tour, 1978. (Retna)

Bottom left: With Pattie, USA, 1978. (Michael Putland)

19
Forest National, Brussels.

20
Jaap Edenhal, Amsterdam.

24
Apollo Theatre, Glasgow. Eric plays Robert Johnson's 'Kindhearted Woman Blues'. Lucky Scots.

25
City Hall, Newcastle-upon-Tyne.

26
Apollo Theatre, Manchester.

28
Victoria Hall, Hanley.

29
Gala Ballroom, West Bromwich.

1978/79

DECEMBER 1978

1
Gaumont Theatre, Southampton.

2
Conference Centre, Brighton.

5, 6
Hammersmith Odeon, London. Muddy Waters joins Eric for the encore.

7
Civic Hall, Guildford. Muddy Waters joins Eric for 'Hey Baby'. George Harrison and Elton John join Eric for 'Further On Up The Road'.
Eric's new album 'Backless' released.

FEBRUARY 1979

'If I Don't Be There By Morning' backed with 'Tulsa Time' released as Eric's new single.
George Harrison releases his 'George Harrison' LP. Eric plays on 'Love Comes To Everyone'.

MARCH 1979

Eric prepares for Irish and American tours. Eric's band now consists of Eric (guitar, vocals), Albert Lee (guitar, vocals), Dick Sims (organ), Carl Radle (bass), Jamie Oldaker (drums).
The set normally runs as follows: 'Badge', 'If I Don't Be There', 'Worried Life Blues', 'Crossroads', 'Knockin' On Heaven's Door', 'Tulsa Time', 'Early In The Morning', 'Watch Out For Lucy', 'Setting Me Up', 'Double Trouble', 'Lay Down Sally', 'Wonderful Tonight', 'Cocaine', 'Layla' and 'Further On Up The Road'.

8
City Hall, Cork.

9
St. John Lynns, Tralee.

11
Leisureland, Galway.

BACKLESS

UK RSO 5001
US RSO RS 1-3039
Released November 1978

Side One:
1. Walk Out In The Rain
2. Watch Out For Lucy
3. I'll Make Love To You
4. Roll It
5. Tell Me That You Love Me
Side Two:
6. If I Don't Be There By Morning
7. Early In The Morning
8. Promises
9. Golden Ring
10. Tulsa Time

Top right: Wedding photograph, March 27, 1979, Tucson, Arizona.

12
Sandy, Limerick.

13
Standhill, Sligo.

15
Downtown Club, Dundalk.

16
Army Drill Hall, Dublin. (This gig was done as a thank you to the Army for helping Eric ship his gear on previous tours.)

17
National Stadium, Dublin.

Eric Clapton: Roger Forrester said to me that certain production type songs like 'Layla' or 'Badge' were songs where it definitely needed a fuller sound, and suggested Albert Lee. And it was just like bang – light bulb – and I thought, why didn't I think of that?

The band rehearse at Ascot race course for a huge American tour.

27
Eric marries Pattie in Tucson, Arizona, before starting his American tour. Muddy Waters is the support act.

28
Community Centre, Tucson, Az. During 'Wonderful Tonight' Eric

brings his bride on stage and dedicates the song to her.

29
Civic Center, Albuquerque, NM.

31
University of Texas Special Events Center, El Paso, Tx.

APRIL 1979

1
Chaparral Center, Midland, Tx.

3
Lloyd Noble Center, Norman, Ok.

4
Hammons Center, Springfield, Ill.

6
Assembly Center, Tulsa, Ok.

7
Convention Center, Pine Bluff, Ark.

9
Summit, Houston, Tx.

10
Tarrant Co. Convention Center, Fort Worth, Tx.

11
Municipal Auditorium, Austin, Tx.

Top left: In Poland, 1979.
(Chris Horler)

Bottom: A restless audience
in Poland, 1979. (Chris
Horler)

1979

12
Convention Center, San Antonio, Tx.

14
Civic Center, Monroe, Mich.

17
Freedom Hall, Johnson City, Tenn.

18
Coliseum, Knoxville, Tenn.

20
University of Atlanta Coliseum, Tuscaloosa, Ga.

21
Omni, Atlanta, Ga.

22
Municipal Auditorium, Mobile, Ala.

24
William and Mary University, Williamsburg, Pa.

25
Mosque, Richmond, Va.

26
Capitol Center, Washington, DC.

28
Civic Center, Providence, RI.

29
Veterans Memorial Coliseum, New Haven, Ct.

30
Spectrum, Philadelphia, Pa. Eric flies home for a break.

MAY 1979
20
Eric and Pattie celebrate their wedding with a huge party at their home. Paul McCartney, Ringo Starr, George Harrison, Denny Laine and Jack Bruce are among the 200 guests

and all play with Eric in a marquee in the grounds of his home.

25
Civic Center, Augusta, Ga.

26
Cumberland County Civic Center, Portland, Or.

28
Civic Center, Birmingham, NY.

29
War Memorial Arena, Syracuse, N.Y.

30
War Memorial, Rochester, N.Y.

JUNE 1979
1
Memorial Auditorium, Buffalo, N.Y.

2
Richfield Coliseum, Cleveland, Oh.

4
Sports Arena, Toledo, Oh.

5
Civic Center, Saginaw, Mich.

7
Riverfront Coliseum, Cincinnati, Oh.

8
Market Square Arena, Indianapolis, Ind.

9
Dane County Exposition Center, Madison, Wi.

10
Civic Center, St. Paul, Minn.

12
Stadium, Chicago, Ill. Eric jams with Muddy Waters on 'Got My Mojo Working'. Muddy Waters and Johnny Winter jam with Eric on 'Long Distance Call' and 'Kansas City'.

Top right: With Muddy Waters, Dingwalls, London, December 1978. (Paul Slattery)

Centre right: At Glyn Johns' wedding, 1978. (LFI)

13
Wings Stadium, Kalamazoo, Mich.

15
Notre Dame University, South Bend, Ind.

16
Brown County Veterans Memorial Coliseum, Green Bay, Mich.

18
Civic Auditorium, Omaha, Ne.

19
Kansas Coliseum, Wichita, Ka.

21
Salt Palace, Salt Lake City, Ut.

23
Coliseum, Spokane, Wa.

24
Coliseum, Seattle, Wa. Marc Benno releases his 'Lost In Austin' LP. Eric plays on 'Hotfoot Blues', 'Chasin' Rainbows', 'Me And A Friend Of Mine', 'New Romance', 'Last Train', 'Lost In Austin', 'Splish Splash', 'Monterey Pen', 'The Drifter', 'Hey There Senorita'.

AUGUST 1979
Danny Douma releases his 'Night Eyes' LP. Eric plays on 'Hate You'.

SEPTEMBER 1979
Eric premières his all new British band which now consists of Albert Lee (guitar and vocals), Henri Spinetti (drums), Dave Markee (bass) and Chris Stainton (keyboards). They embark on a world tour.

30
Victoria Hall, Hanley. The sets include the following songs: 'Badge', 'Worried Life Blues', 'If I Don't Be There By Morning', 'Tulsa Time', 'Early In The Morning', 'Watch Out For Lucy', 'Wonderful Tonight', 'Setting Me Up', 'La La La', 'Lay Down Sally', 'All Our Past Times', 'Double Trouble', 'After Midnight', 'Knockin' On Heaven's Door', 'Country Boy', 'Key To The Highway', 'Cocaine', 'Further On Up The Road' and 'Blues Power'.

OCTOBER 1979
6
Stadthalle, Vienna.

7
Sporthalle, Linz.

8
Messehalle, Nuremberg. The tour continues in Yugoslavia and Poland: The Palata Pioneer Hall in Belgrade, two shows at The Dom Sportover in Zagreb, The Palace Of Culture in Warsaw and The Katowice Stadium

in Katowice which was a disastrous concert for Eric due to police brutality towards fans.

Eric Clapton: **How can I play when I see kids right in front of the stage, underneath me, being pushed about by the men from Sainsbury's. Anywhere else in the world we could help the kids by telling them to cool it. But there, I'm powerless because of the language problem and because the authorities are so heavy. The whole place reminds me of the Third Man.**

The tour continues to Israel with three shows at the Mann Auditorium, Tel Aviv, and one at The Binianei Hadoma in Jerusalem. Eric and his band then take a two week break back home.

NOVEMBER 1979
The tour resumes and continues in Thailand at the National Theatre in Bangkok, followed by a show in the Philippines capital of Manila.

20
Academic Community Hall, Hong Kong. The tour continues with 10 dates in Japan.

23
Japan (Ibaragi).

25
Japan (Nagoya).

26
Japan.

27
Japan.

28
Japan.

30
Japan.

DECEMBER 1979
1
Koseinkin Hall, Osaka, Japan.

73

1980/81

3, 4

Budokan, Tokyo, Japan. (Live recording of 'Just One Night'.)

6

Japan.

FEBRUARY 1980

Gary Brooker releases 'Home Lovin'' backed with 'Chasing The Chop'. Eric plays on both.

MARCH 1980

Alexis Korner releases his 'Party Album'. Eric plays on 'Hey Pretty Mama', 'Hi Heel Sneakers' and 'They Call It Stormy Monday'. This double album is only released in Germany.

APRIL 1980

Gary Brooker joins Eric's band. Recording begins at Surrey Sound Studios.

Gary Brooker releases 'Leave The Candle' as a single. Eric plays on the A-side.

MAY 1980

British tour opens in Oxford. The set normally runs as follows: 'Tulsa Time', 'Early In The Morning', 'Lay Down Sally', 'Wonderful Tonight', 'Country Boy', 'Thunder And Lightning', 'Blues Power', 'All Our Pastimes', 'Setting Me Up', 'Leave The Candle', 'If I Don't Be There By Morning', 'Ramblin' On My Mind', 'Have You Ever Loved A Woman', 'After Midnight', 'Cocaine', 'Layla' and 'Further On Up The Road'.

2

New Theatre, Oxford.

3

Brighton Centre, Brighton.

4

Bingley Hall, Stafford.

7

City Hall, Newcastle-upon-Tyne.

8

Odeon, Edinburgh.

Top right: Posing for sleeve shot of 'Just One Night'.

JUST ONE NIGHT

UK RSDX 2
US RSO RS 2-4202
Released May 1980

Side One:
1. Tulsa Time
2. Early In The Morning
3. Lay Down Sally
4. Wonderful Tonight
Side Two:
5. If I Don't Be There By Morning
6. Worried Life Blues
7. All Our Past Times
8. After Midnight
Side Three:
9. Double Trouble
10. Setting Me Up
11. Blues Power
Side Four:
12. Ramblin' On My Mind
13. Cocaine
14. Further On Up The Road

9

Apollo, Glasgow.

11

Leisure Centre, Deeside.

12

Coventry Theatre, Coventry.

.13

Hippodrome, Bristol.

15, 16, 17

Hammersmith Odeon, London.

18

Civic Hall, Guildford. Jeff Beck jams with Eric on 'Ramblin' On My Mind'. Eric and Albert Lee jam with Chas and Dave on 'Roll Over Beethoven'. Chas and Dave support Eric on the tour.

Eric releases his live double LP 'Just One Night' recorded at the Budokan, Tokyo, December 1979.

JULY 1980

Ronnie Lane releases his 'See Me' LP. Eric plays on 'Lad's Got Money', 'Barcelona' and 'Way Up Yonder'.

Eric and band head off to Compass Point Studios in Nassau to begin recording a new studio LP.

SEPTEMBER 1980

Scandinavian tour. Band is same as British tour.

19

Aalborghall, Allborg.

20

Broendbyhall, Copenhagen.

21

Vejlbyrisskovhall, Aarhus.

23

Olympen, Lund.

24

Scandinavium, Gothenberg.

25

Drammenshall, Oslo.

27

Isstadion, Stockholm.

29

Messhall, Helsinki.

JANUARY 1981

Start of short Irish tour. 'Whiter Shade Of Pale' added to the set.

31

R.D.S., Dublin.

FEBRUARY 1981

1

Galway.

Left: Poland, 1979. (Chris Horler)

1981

Top and centre right: At The Secret Policeman's Other Ball, Drury Lane Theatre, London, September 1981. (Michael Putland)

ANOTHER TICKET

UK RSO 5008
US RSO RX 1-3095
Released February 1981

Side One:
1. Something Special
2. Black Rose
3. Blow Wind Blow
4. Another Ticket
5. I Can't Stand It
Side Two:
6. Hold Me Lord
7. Floating Bridge
8. Catch Me If You Can
9. Rita Mae

2
Cork.

3
U.R.I., Carlow.

25
Rainbow, London. Eric releases 'I Can't Stand It' backed with 'Black Rose' as a single.

Eric also releases a new album 'Another Ticket'.

Phil Collins releases his 'Face Value' LP. Eric plays on 'If Leaving Me Is Easy'.

MARCH 1981
Start of huge U.S. tour which is cut short due to illness.
'Rita Mae' added to the set.

2
Memorial Coliseum, Portland, Ore.

3
The Coliseum, Spokane, Wa.

5, 6, 7
Paramount Theater, Seattle, Wa.

9
Yellowstone Metra, Billings, Mont.

10
The Four Seasons Arena, Great Falls, Mont.

13
Dane County Exposition Centre, Madison, Wi.

14
Eric is rushed to hospital for treatment for ulcers, one of which is later described by doctors as 'as big as an orange'. Forty-seven concerts are cancelled. Eric was seriously ill, very close to dying, and would not reappear in public until September.

APRIL 1981
Eric releases 'Another Ticket' backed with 'Rita Mae' as a single.

SEPTEMBER 1981
Charity concerts for Amnesty International:

9
Theatre Royal, Drury Lane, London. Eric plays with Jeff Beck on 'Cause We Ended As Lovers' and 'Crossroads'.

They join the rest of the artists for 'I Shall Be Released'.

10
Theatre Royal, Drury Lane, London. Eric plays with Jeff Beck on 'Cause We Ended As Lovers' and 'Further On Up The Road'. They join the rest of the artists for 'I Shall Be Released'.

12
Theatre Royal, Drury Lane, London. Eric and Jeff Beck join the other artists for 'I Shall Be Released'.

Other musicians appearing at these shows include Midge Ure, Sting, Donovan and Phil Collins. Comedians include Billy Connolly, John Cleese, Rowan Atkinson,

Pamela Stephenson and Alexi Sayle.

John Martyn releases his 'Glorious Fool' LP. Eric plays on 'Couldn't Love You More'.

Stack-O-Hits Records release 'All Night Boogie' by Howlin' Wolf. This gem consists of outtakes from 'The London Sessions'. Eric plays on all tracks.

OCTOBER 1981

The set for the upcoming Scandinavian tour runs as follows: 'Tulsa Time', 'Lay Down Sally', 'Wonderful Tonight', 'Worried Life Blues', 'After Midnight', 'Whiter Shade Of Pale', 'Country Boy', 'Double Trouble', 'Rita Mae', 'Knockin' On Heaven's Door', 'Blues Power', 'Ramblin' On My Mind'/ 'Have You Ever Loved A Woman', 'Cocaine', 'Layla' and 'Further On Up The Road'.

7

Messhall, Helsinki.

9

Isstadion, Stockholm.

10

Scandinavium, Gothenburg.

12

Drammenshall, Oslo.

13

Olympen, Lund.

15

Broendbyhall, Copenhagen.

16

Vejlbyrissnovhall, Aarhus.

17

Randers Hallen, Randers. Eric plays saxophone on 'Further On Up The Road' and renames 'Cocaine' 'Cornflakes'.

NOVEMBER 1981

16

Civic Hall, Wolverhampton. Eric plays one off gig for the John Wile testimonial before heading off to tour Japan.

30

Koseinkin Hall, Nagoya, Japan.

DECEMBER 1981

1

Osaka, Japan.

4

Kyoto, Japan.

7

Osaka, Japan.

8

Yokahama, Japan.

Centre far left: Rehearsals for The Secret Policeman's Other Ball with Jeff Beck and Sting. (Michael Putland).

Bottom far left: SPOB with Jeff Beck and Neil Murray. (Michael Putland)

Left: Backstage at Drury Lane, September 1981, with Sting and Jeff Beck. (Adrian Boot)

1982

9
Tokyo, Japan.

MARCH 1982
A very quiet year for Eric which is spent curing his drink problem and restoring his health.

Eric Clapton: **It was pointed out to me while I was in hospital that I had a drink problem, and I think that was the first time anyone had ever said something like that to me. But I was still happy drinking and quite terrified of not drinking. I had to go further down that road to complete insanity before I stopped.**

Gary Brooker releases his 'Lead Me To The Water' LP. Eric plays on the title track.
'The Secret Policeman's Other Ball – The Music' LP released. Eric plays on 'Cause We Ended As Lovers', 'Further On Up The Road', 'Crossroads' and 'I Shall Be Released'.

MAY 1982
18
Eric is interviewed on BBC1 after his horse *The Ripleyite* wins the three o'clock at Goodwood races.
Eric attends a Ry Cooder show at Hammersmith Odeon in London.

JUNE 1982
Eric undertakes his one and only tour of the year. The band is unchanged and the set runs as follows: 'Tulsa Time', 'Lay Down Sally', 'I Shot The Sheriff', 'Blow Wind Blow', 'Wonderful Tonight', 'Pink Bedroom', 'Whiter Shade Of Pale', 'Key To The Highway', 'Double Trouble', 'Blues Power', 'Cocaine', 'Layla' and 'Further On Up The Road'.

5
Paramount Theater, Cedar Rapids, Mich.

6
Civic Auditorium, Omaha, Ne.

7
Metropolitan Center, Minneapolis, Minn.

10, 11
Pine Knob Pavilion, Detroit, Mich.

12
Memorial Auditorium, Buffalo, N.Y.

13
Blossom Music Center, Cleveland, Oh.

17
Cumberland County Civic Center, Portland, Me.

18
Broome County Coliseum, Binghampton, NY.

19
Performing Arts Center, Saratoga, NY.

22
Hampton Roads Coliseum, Hampton, NY.

23
Coliseum, Charlotte, N.Ca.

24
Viking Hall, Bristol, Tenn.

27
Civic Center, Augusta, Ga.

28
Coliseum, Jacksonville, Fl.

29
Civic Center, Lakeland, Fl.

30
Sportatorium, Miami, Fl. Muddy Waters jams with Eric on 'Blow Wind Blow'. Sadly, this turned out to be Muddy's last live appearance.

SEPTEMBER, OCTOBER, NOVEMBER 1982
Eric replaces his English rhythm section with American musicians.

Eric records his new LP at Compass Point Studios, Nassau, with Duck Dunn (bass), Roger Hawkins (drums), Albert Lee (guitar, keyboards) and Ry Cooder (guitar).

DECEMBER 1982
22
Eric plays The Royal Pub in Guildford, Surrey.

1983

JANUARY 1983

Eric rehearses with his new band for a huge tour. Chris Stainton rejoins the group.

'I've Got A Rock 'n' Roll Heart' backed with 'Man In Love' released as Eric's new single.

FEBRUARY 1983

Eric's band now features Duck Dunn (bass), Roger Hawkins (drums), Albert Lee (guitar, keyboards) and Chris Stainton (keyboards). Ry Cooder is support act for the U.S. tour.

The set for the first half of the tour is as follows: 'After Midnight', 'I Shot The Sheriff', 'Worried Life Blues', 'Crazy Country Hop', 'Crosscut Saw', 'Slow Down Linda', 'Sweet Little Lisa', 'Key To The Highway', 'Tulsa Time', 'Rock'n'Roll Heart', 'Wonderful Tonight', 'Blues Power', 'Who's Lovin' You Tonight', 'Have You Ever Loved A Woman', 'Ramblin' On My Mind', 'Let It Rain', 'Cocaine', 'Layla' and 'Further On Up The Road'.

MONEY AND CIGARETTES

UK W 3773
US Warner Bros/Duck Records 123773
Released February 1983

Side One:
1. Everybody Oughta Make A Change
2. The Shape You're In
3. Aren't Going Down
4. I've Got A Rock'n'Roll Heart
5. Man Overboard
Side Two:
6. Pretty Girl
7. Man In Love
8. Crosscut Saw
9. Slow Down Linda
10. Crazy Country Hop

The tour is promoted by Camel cigarettes, which causes various health-related organisations to complain.

Nat Walker (Camel Cigarettes): We felt that the music of a guy like Eric Clapton fits the interest profile of a Camel smoker. Music is important to the Camel brand.

1, 2

Paramount Theatre, Seattle. Eric plays 'Pretty Girl' and 'Nobody Knows You When You're Down And Out' during his set.

3

Cumberland County Civic Center, Portland, Ore.

6

Convention Center, Sacramento, Ca.

7

Cow Palace, San Francisco, Ca.

8

Universal Amphitheater, Los Angeles, Ca.

9

Arena, Long Beach, Ca.

11

Veterans Memorial Coliseum, Phoenix, Ar.

13

Erwin Events Center, Austin, Tx.

14

The Summit, Houston, Tx.

15

Reunion Arena, Dallas, Tx. Last show with Roger Hawkins. He is replaced by Jamie Oldaker.

17

Mid South Coliseum, Memphis, Tenn.

18

Kiel Auditorium, St. Louis, Mo.

19

Metro Centre, Rockford, Ill.

21

Spectrum, Philadelphia, Pa. Ry Cooder jams with Eric on 'Crossroads'.

22

Brendan Byrne Arena, East Rutherford, N.J.

25

Omni, Atlanta, Ga.

26

The Gardens, Louisville, Ky.

28

Capital Center, Washington, D.C. Eric's new LP. 'Money And Cigarettes' is released.

MARCH 1983

1

Centrum, Worcester, Mass.

2

Hershey Park Arena, Hershey, Pa.

3

Civic Arena, Pittsburgh, Pa. 'The Shape You're In' backed with 'Crosscut Saw' released as Eric's new single.

APRIL 1983

Start of British and European tour before continuing in the U.S. The set is as follows: 'Tulsa Time', 'I Shot The Sheriff', 'Worried Life Blues', 'Lay Down Sally', 'Let It Rain', 'Double Trouble', 'Sweet Little Lisa', 'Key To The Highway', 'After Midnight', 'The Shape You're In', 'Wonderful Tonight', 'Blues Power',

'Ramblin' On My Mind', 'Have You Ever Loved A Woman', 'Cocaine', 'Layla', and 'Further On Up The Road'.

8, 9

Playhouse, Edinburgh.

11

City Hall, Newcastle-upon-Tyne.

12

Empire, Liverpool.

14, 15, 16

National Stadium, Dublin.

20

Stadthalle, Bremen.

21

Grugahalle, Essen.

23

Ahoy Hall, Rotterdam.

24

Chapitau De Pantin, Paris.

26

Sportshalle, Cologne.

27

Festhalle, Frankfurt.

29

Rhein Neckar Halle, Eppelheim.

30

St. Jakobshalle, Basle.

MAY 1983

2

Palasport, Rome.

Above left: Hammersmith Odeon, May 1983. (Barry Plummer)

1983

3

Palasport, Genoa.

13

Coliseum, St. Austell

14

Arts Centre, Poole.

16, 17, 18, 19

Hammersmith Odeon, London.

21

Apollo, Manchester.

22

De Montfort Hall, Leicester.

23

Civic Hall, Guildford. This is another of the very special home town shows that Eric occasionally plays for his family, friends and locals.

The set is 'Tulsa Time', 'I Shot The Sheriff', 'Worried Life Blues', 'Lay Down Sally', 'Let It Rain', 'Double Trouble', 'Sweet Little Lisa', 'The Shape You're In', 'Wonderful Tonight', 'Blues Power', 'Sad Sad Day', 'Have You Ever Loved A Woman', 'Ramblin' On My Mind' and 'Layla'.

Encores of 'Further On Up The Road' and 'Cocaine' feature Phil Collins (drums) and Jimmy Page (guitar). 'Roll Over Beethoven' follows with Chas and Dave, followed by 'You Won Again', 'Matchbox' and 'Goodnight Irene' with Paul Brady joining the rest of this special ad-hoc band.

'Slow Down Linda' backed with 'Crazy Country Hop' is released as Eric's new single.

JUNE 1983

5

New Victoria Theatre, London. Joins Chas and Dave, Richard Digance and Jim Davidson for a Save The Children benefit.

24

Eric is presented with this year's Silver Clef award for Outstanding Achievement in the World of British Music by Princess Michael of Kent at the eighth Music Therapy Charity lunch in London.

25

Kingswood Music Theater, Toronto, Can.

27, 28, 29

Pine Knob Pavilion, Detroit, Mich. Ringo Starr releases his 'Old Wave' album. Eric plays on 'Everybody's In A Hurry But Me'.

JULY 1983

1

Performing Arts Center, Saratoga, NY.

2, 3

Jones Beach, Wantaugh, NY.

5

Coliseum, Columbia, S. Cal.

7

Blossom Music Center, Cleveland, Oh.

9

Civic Center Arena, St. Paul, Minn.

10

Summerfest, Milwaukee, Wi.

11

Poplar Creek, Chicago, Ill. After this show Eric goes to the Checker Board lounge where he jams with Buddy Guy.

13

Kings Islands, Cincinnati, Oh.

16, 17

Red Rocks, Denver, Co. On the 17th, The Blasters join Eric on 'Further On Up The Road'.

Eric Clapton: I am much more out front now, and I do feel much more confident. I know what I can do, yet I know my limits. When I'm playing well it knocks me out.

All shots from
Hammersmith Odeon, May
1983. (Barry Plummer)

1983

AUGUST 1983

The press announce that Eric will be doing two charity shows in September to celebrate twenty years in the business.

Eric helps out Roger Waters, formerly of Pink Floyd, for the recording of his 'Pros And Cons Of Hitch-Hiking' LP.

SEPTEMBER 1983
20

Royal Albert Hall, London (Ronnie Lane/Arms Benefits). The set for this show is 'Everybody Oughta Make A Change', 'Lay Down Sally', 'Wonderful Tonight', 'Ramblin' On My Mind', 'Have You Ever Loved A Woman', 'Rita Mae', 'Cocaine' and 'Man Smart Woman Smarter'. Eric then accompanies Stevie Winwood on 'Hound Dog', 'Best That I Can', 'Road Runner', 'Slowdown Sundown', 'Take Me To The River' and 'Gimme Some Lovin''.

After an interval Jeff Beck performs 'Star Cycle', 'Pump', 'Led Boots', 'Goodbye Pork Pie Hat', 'People Get Ready' and 'Hi Ho Silver Lining', and Jimmy Page performs 'Prelude', 'Who's To Blame', 'City Sirens', and 'Stairway To Heaven'. Neither Beck's nor Page's set feature Eric. After Page's last number, Eric and Jeff Beck return to the stage for the remainder of the show together with Jimmy Page. They perform 'Tulsa Time', 'Wee Wee Baby' and 'Layla'. Ronnie Lane comes out for the final two numbers, 'Bomber's Moon' and 'Goodnight Irene'.

A very emotional and historic night which is videoed for later release.

21

Royal Albert Hall, London (Prince's Trust). Eric's set for this show is: 'Everybody Oughta Make A Change', 'Lay Down Sally', 'Ramblin' On My Mind', 'Have You Ever Loved A Woman', 'Rita Mae', 'Cocaine', and 'Man Smart Woman Smarter'. Eric's set is followed by Stevie Winwood performing 'The Best That I Can', 'Road Runner', 'Slowdown Sundown', 'Take Me To The River' and 'Gimme Some Lovin'', all featuring Eric. Jeff Beck's and Jimmy Page's sets follow. The whole band return for: 'Wee Wee Baby' and 'Layla'. Ronnie Lane comes out for the final number, 'Goodnight Irene'.

A much shorter set than the previous night, probably because Prince Charles and Princess Diana are in the Royal Box. It's still a great show though.

The backing band for these two shows comprises: Andy Fairweather Low (guitar, vocals), Kenney Jones (drums), Charlie Watts (drums), Bill Wyman (bass), Ray Cooper (percussion), Chris Stainton (keyboards), James Hooker (keyboards), Fernando Saunders (bass) and Simon Phillips (drums).

Eric Clapton: **Obviously it was a concert I very much wanted to do both on behalf of Ronnie (Lane), and on behalf of the Action Research into Multiple Sclerosis Fund. But that didn't mean I wasn't nervous. Far from it, I was petrified when we had the first rehearsals. But it rapidly became great fun. And it was a delight to work with such a competent bunch of musicians.**

Originally, the idea was for everyone to just sort of loosely jam together, but subsequently it was quite rightly decided that everyone involved should do their own little regular sets, with the rest of the band providing the backing.

Top right: At the Royal Albert Hall ARMS concert, September 21, 1983. (LFI)

Centre, right: RAH Arms concert, September 20, 1983, with Bill Wyman. (Andre Csillag)

Bottom right: RAH Arms show, September 20, with Bill Wyman and Jeff Beck. (Andre Csillag)

OCTOBER 1983

The press announce the Albert Hall supergroup will do a short tour of America for ARMS.

Bill Wyman: We all had such a great time at the Albert Hall we decided to carry on. We thought it would have been a shame to have simply gone our separate ways. The meeting was much easier to arrange than any I've had with the Stones. We were all there bang on eleven o'clock. With the Stones eleven o'clock on Wednesday usually means nine o'clock on Friday.

NOVEMBER 1983

Eric attends the opening of The Hippodrome amongst a host of stars. Stevie Winwood is unable to do the U.S. ARMS dates and is replaced by Joe Cocker. Paul Rogers also joins the line-up as does Jan Hammer. The backing band remains the same as for the Albert Hall.

The set for the U.S. shows runs as follows: 'Everybody Oughta Make A Change', 'Lay Down Sally', 'Wonderful Tonight', 'Rita Mae', 'Sad Sad Day', 'Have You Ever Loved A Woman', 'Ramblin' On My Mind' and 'Cocaine'. Eric's set is followed by

Joe Cocker performing 'Don't Talk To Me', 'Watching The River Flow', 'Worried Life Blues', 'You Are So Beautiful', 'Seven Days' and 'Feelin' Alright'. Eric is featured on all. Jeff Beck follows as does Jimmy Page who performs 'Stairway To Heaven' at the end of his set. Unlike in England, he is joined by Jeff Beck and Eric for some great guitar duelling during Led Zeppelin's anthem. The whole band return to perform 'Layla', and 'With A Little Help From My Friends'. Ronnie Lane comes out to perform 'April Fool' and 'Goodnight Irene' accompanied by the whole cast.

28, 29

Reunion Arena, Dallas, Tx. After the show, Eric goes to the Tango Club in Dallas with Bill Wyman to jam with Lonnie Mack.

DECEMBER 1983
1, 2, 3

Cow Palace, San Francisco, Ca.

5, 6

Forum, Los Angeles, Ca. After the show, Eric, Jeff Beck and Ron Wood go to the Baked Potato Club to watch Duane Eddy.

1983/84

8, 9

Madison Square Garden, New York, N.Y. Ronnie Wood joins Eric on 'Cocaine' and the encores.

Bill Graham: **Neal Schon (of Journey) was here last night, and he said, 'Bill – we should do this. The young musicians. We could get Carlos Santana and Eddie Van Halen and myself together...' And I said, 'Come onnnnn, are you kidding? Which part would you play?'**

JANUARY 1984
15, 16, 17, 18

Eric rehearses for an upcoming tour.
   The set for this tour is as follows: 'Everybody Oughta Make A Change', 'Motherless Children', 'I Shot The Sheriff', 'The Sky Is Crying', 'Badge', 'The Shape You're In', 'Same Old Blues', 'Rita Mae', 'Blow Wind Blow', 'Wonderful

Tonight', 'Let It Rain', 'Key To The Highway', 'Sweet Little Lisa', 'Double Trouble', 'Tulsa Time', 'Bottle Of Red Wine', 'Honey Bee', 'Have You Ever Loved A Woman', 'Ramblin' On My Mind', 'Cocaine', 'Layla' and 'Further On Up The Road'.
   The band is the same as the 1983 tour.

20, 21

Hallenstadion, Zurich.

23, 24

Teatrotenda, Milan.

26

Beogradski-Sajam Hala, Belgrade.

28, 29

Sporting of Athens, Athens.

All shots from Roger Waters' tour, June 1984. (Barry Plummer)

FEBRUARY 1984
2
American University, Cairo.

5, 6
B'Nai Haooma, Jerusalem.

7
Returns to England.

MARCH 1984
Eric flies to Montserrat with (producer) Phil Collins for the recording of his next LP.

Tracks that Eric records are: 'Too Bad', 'She's Waiting', 'Same Old Blues', 'Knock On Wood', 'It All Depends', 'Tangled In Love', 'Never Make You Cry', 'Just Like A Prisoner', 'Jailbreak', 'Heaven's Just One Step Away', 'You Don't Know Like I Know' (a duet with Phil Collins).

APRIL 1984
More recording at Montserrat Air Studios. Roger Waters releases his 'Pros And Cons Of Hitch-Hiking' LP. Eric plays on all tracks.

MAY 1984
Rehearsals for the forthcoming Roger Waters tour.

JUNE 1984
The band for the Roger Waters tour comprises Waters (bass, vocals), Tim Renwick (guitar), Michael Kamen (keyboards), Andy Newmark (drums), Mel Collins (sax), Doreen Chanter (backing vocals), Katie Kissoon (backing vocals), Chris Stainton (keyboards) and Eric Clapton (guitar, vocals).

The set for the tour is as follows: Part 1 – 'Set The Controls For The Heart Of The Sun', 'Money', 'If', 'Welcome To The Machine', 'Have A Cigar', 'Wish You Were Here', 'Pigs On The Wing', 'In The Flesh', 'Nobody Home', 'Hey You' and 'The Gunner's Dream'. Part 2 – '4.30 a.m. (Apparently They Were Travelling Abroad)', '4.33 a.m. (Running Shoes)', '4.37 a.m. (Arabs With Knives And West German Skies)',

1984

Right: With Roger Waters. (Barry Plummer)

'4.39 a.m. (For The First Time Today – Part 2)', '4.41 a.m. (Sexual Revolution)', '4.47 a.m. (The Remains Of Our Love)', '4.50 a.m. (Go Fishing)', '4.56 a.m. (For The First Time Today – Part 1)', '4.58 a.m. (Dunroamin, Duncarin, Dunlivin)', '5.01 a.m. (The Pros And Cons Of Hitch Hiking)', '5.06 a.m. (Every Stranger's Eyes)', '5.11 a.m. (The Moment Of Clarity)'. The encore is 'Brain Damage'.

Eric undertakes this tour against the wishes of his management, but to an outsider it provides the listener with some of his finest playing because he is not under the pressure of being permanently in the spotlight.

16, 17
Isstadion, Stockholm.

19
Ahoy Theatre, Rotterdam.

21, 22
Earls Court, London.

26, 27
N.E.C., Birmingham. Corey Hart releases his solo LP. Eric plays on 'Jenny Fey'.

JULY 1984
3
Hallenstadium, Zurich.

6
Palais Des Sport, Paris. End of tour. U.S. tour to follow.

7
Wembley Stadium, London. Eric jams with Bob Dylan alongside Carlos Santana, Chrissie Hynde, Van Morrison and Mick Taylor on 'Leopard Skin Pillbox Hat', 'It's All Over Now Baby Blue', 'Tombstone Blues', 'Senor', 'The Times They Are A Changin'', 'Blowin' In The Wind' and 'Knockin' On Heaven's Door'.

Eric attends the launch of 'The Ronnie Lane Appeal For Arms Concert' video at a London hotel together with Bill Wyman, Andy Fairweather Low, Kenny Jones, Stevie Winwood and Ronnie Lane.

17, 18
Civic Center, Hartford, Ct.

U.S. leg of the Roger Waters' tour.

20, 21, 22
Meadowlands Arena, New Jersey.

24
Spectrum, Philadephia, Pa.

26
Stadium, Chicago, Ill.

28, 29
Maple Leaf Gardens, Toronto, Canada.

31
The Forum, Montreal, Canada. Although Roger Waters plays further American dates the following year, Eric has by this time left his band.

AUGUST 1984
4
Phil Collins marries. The marquee in the back of his garden finds Collins

jamming with Eric, Robert Plant and Peter Gabriel.

OCTOBER 1984
Eric spends most of the month rehearsing for his upcoming Australasian tour. Albert Lee is no longer in the band.

NOVEMBER 1984
Eric's band now comprises: Eric (guitar, vocals), Chris Stainton (keyboards), Jamie Oldaker (drums), Duck Dunn (bass), Marcy Levy (backing vocals), Shaun Murphy (backing vocals) and Peter Robinson (synthesizer).

The set for the tour is as follows: 'Everybody Oughta Make A Change', 'Motherless Children', 'I Shot The Sheriff', 'Same Old Blues', 'Tangled In Love', 'She's Waiting', 'Steppin' Out', 'Tulsa Time', 'Badge', 'Love Sign', 'Wonderful Tonight', 'Let It Rain', 'Who's Loving You Tonight', 'Have You Ever Loved A Woman', 'Ramblin' On My Mind', 'Cocaine', 'Layla', 'Knock On Wood' and 'You Don't Know Like I Know'.

13, 14
Hordern Pavilion, Sydney.

17
Festival Hall, Brisbane.

20, 21
Hordern Pavilion, Sydney.

23, 24, 25
Sports and Entertainments Centre, Melbourne.

28
Entertainments Centre, Perth. 'You Don't Know Like I Know', a duet with Eric and Phil Collins, released in Australia to coincide with the tour. It has not been released elsewhere.

An amusing incident happens in Perth. Angry at being woken at some ungodly hour by Ritchie Blackmore's impromptu jam session in the Sheraton Hotel, Eric sends his minder Alfie to sort things out. Shouldering his way into Ritchie's room, he warns 'If I have to come

Top left: With Pattie at The Hippodrome opening, 1984. (Eugene Adebari)

Bottom far left: (LFI)

Left: With Marcy Levy.(LFI)

1984/85

back here there's going to be a stoush'. Needless to say, silence reigned supreme. Alfie's stature is rather on the large side.

DECEMBER 1984
2
The Coliseum, Hong Kong. End of tour.

Eric attends one of Nik Kershaw's concerts at Hammersmith Odeon.

JANUARY 1985
2
Eric attends Ronnie Wood's wedding in Denham. Eric films his first ever video for an upcoming single 'Forever Man'.

FEBRUARY 1985
17
Attends première of Terry Gilliam's film *Brazil*.

FEBRUARY 1985
18
Eric rehearses for his upcoming world tour. Tim Renwick is added to the band on guitar and Peter Robinson leaves.

The set for the British and Scandinavian tour is as follows:

Top right and below: Wembley Arena, March 4, 1985. (Stuart Pearsall).

Bottom right: With Pattie at the premiere of *Brazil*. (LFI)

'Everybody Oughta Make a Change', 'Motherless Children', 'I Shot The Sheriff', 'Same Old Blues', 'Blues Power', 'Tangled In Love', 'Steppin' Out', 'Just Like A Prisoner', 'Tulsa Time', 'Something Is Wrong With My Baby', 'Badge', 'Behind The Sun', 'Wonderful Tonight', 'Let It Rain', 'Who's Lovin' You Tonight', 'Have You Ever Loved A Woman', 'Ramblin' On My Mind', 'Cocaine', 'Layla', 'Knock On Wood' and 'Further On Up The Road'.

This whole tour sees Eric playing at his volatile best; in fact he's never played better.

27, 28
The Playhouse, Edinburgh. 'Forever Man' backed with 'Too Bad' released as Eric's new single. 12" has extra track, 'Heaven Is One Step Away'.

MARCH 1985
1, 2
N.E.C., Birmingham. 'Lay Down Sally' replaces 'Just Like A Prisoner' from 2/2/85 onwards.

4, 5
Wembley Arena, London. On The 5th Dan Akroyd jams with Eric on 'Further On Up The Road'. 'You Don't Know Like I Know' added after 'Knock On Wood'.

9
Icehall, Helsinki.

11
Scandinavium, Gothenburg.

12
Valbyhallen, Copenhagen.

14
Drammenshallen, Oslo.

15
Isstadion, Stockholm. Eric's new LP 'Behind The Sun' released; a fine album containing some of Eric's best guitar solos on record, particularly 'Just Like A Prisoner'.

Phil Collins: I think this album will surprise a lot of people. Eric took a Prophet and a Linn away to write the demos which is very unusual for him. He's also singing and playing better than I've ever heard him.

APRIL 1985
Start of American tour. The set for the first part of the American tour is as follows: 'Tulsa Time', 'Motherless Children', 'I Shot The Sheriff', 'Same Old Blues', 'Blues Power', 'Tangled In Love', 'Behind The Sun', 'Wonderful Tonight', 'Steppin' Out', 'Never Make You Cry', 'She's Waiting', 'Something's Wrong With My Baby', 'Lay Down Sally', 'Badge', 'Let It Rain', 'Double Trouble', 'Cocaine', 'Layla', 'Forever Man' and 'Further On Up The Road'.

9
Reunion Arena, Dallas, Tx.

10
The Summit, Houston, Tx.

Left: USA, April 1985.
(Retna)

1985

Right: Wembley Arena, March 4, 1985. (David Redfern)

BEHIND THE SUN

UK Duck Records 925 166-1
US Warner Bros/Duck Records
125661
Released March 1985

Side One:
1. She's Waiting
2. See What Love Can Do
3. Same Old Blues
4. Knock On Wood
5. Something's Happening
Side Two:
6. Forever Man
7. It All Depends
8. Tangled In Love
9. Never Make You Cry
10.Just Like A Prisoner
11.Behind The Sun

11
Erwin Events Center, Austin, Tx.

13
Civic Center, Pensacola, Fl.

15
Civic Center, Lakeland, Fl. George Terry jams with his old boss.

16
James L. Knight Center, Miami, Fl.

18
Duke University, Durham, NC.

19
Civic Center, Savannah, Ga.

20
The Omni, Atlanta, Ga. 'Forever Man' played live for the first time.

22
Coliseum, Richmond, Va.

23
Civic Center, Baltimore, Md. This show is recorded for radio broadcast.

25
Meadowlands Arena, East Rutherford, N.J.

26
Nassau Coliseum, Uniondale, N.J.

28
Civic Center, Providence, R.I. Dick Simms jams with his old boss.

29
The Spectrum, Philadelphia, Pa.

MAY 1985
1
Civic Center, Hertford, Ct.

2
Civic Center, Portland, Me.

3
Forum, Montreal, Canada.

8
Appears on David Letterman Show and performs 'Layla', 'Lay Down Sally', 'White Room', 'Same Old Blues', 'Forever Man' and 'Knock On Wood' with the house band.

His performance of 'White Room', the first time since Cream, inspires Eric to include it in his set for the second part of his tour.

The soundtrack to 'Water' is released. Eric plays on 'Freedom' alongside George Harrison.

The set for the second part of the U.S. tour is as follows: 'Tulsa Time', 'Motherless Children', 'I Shot The Sheriff', 'Same Old Blues', 'Tangled In Love', 'White Room', 'Steppin' Out', 'Wonderful Tonight', 'She's Waiting', 'She Loves You', 'Badge', 'Let It Rain', 'Double Trouble', 'Cocaine', 'Layla', 'Forever Man' and 'Further On Up The Road'.

21
Kingswood Music Theater, Toronto, Canada.

22
Blossom Music Theater, Cleveland, Oh.

23
Finger Lakes Music Center, Canandiagua, NY.

25
Performing Arts Center, Saratoga, NY.

26
The Centrum, Worcester, Mass.

27
Merriweather Post Pavilion, Columbia.

28
Garden State Arts Center, Holmdel, NJ.

30
Summerfest, Milwaukee, Wi. 'She's Waiting' backed with 'Jail Bait' released as Eric's new single.

JULY 1985
2, 3
Pine Knob Pavilion, Detroit, Mi.

5
Poplar Green Music Theater, Chicago, Ill. After this show Eric jams with Buddy Guy for three sets at the Checker Board Lounge. (Anyone got tapes? That must have been something to see and hear..).

6
Music Amphitheater, Indianapolis, Ind.

7
Riverbend Music Theater, Cincinnati, Oh.

9
Sandstone Amphitheater, Kansas City, Ka.

11
Red Rocks Amphitheater, Denver, Co.

13
JFK Stadium, Philadelphia, Pa. This is the historic Live Aid Show. Eric plays 'White Room', 'She's Waiting' and 'Layla' to millions. Eric also joins in the finale of 'We Are The World' and adds some nice guitar lines.

14
Red Rocks Amphitheater, Denver, Co.

17, 18, 19
Universal Amphitheater, Los Angeles, Ca. (Sergio Pastora jams with his old boss on the last night).

21
Compton Terrace, Phoenix, Ar.

22
Pacific Amphitheater, Costa Mesa, Ca.

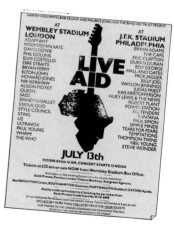

Top left: Backstage at the Live Aid concert, Philadelphia, July 13, 1985. (Retna)

Bottom: (LFI)

93

23, 24

Concord Pavilion, Concord, Ca. Carlos Santana jams with Eric on the first night.

26

Center Coliseum, Seattle, Wash.

27

PNE Coliseum, Canada. Lionel Richie jams with Eric on 'Knock On Wood'. After the show Lionel invites Eric to contribute a guitar track for his upcoming solo LP.

Singer Marcy Levy is replaced by Laura Creamer for the remainder of the world tour.

AUGUST 1985

Month off.

SEPTEMBER 1985

Gary Brooker releases his 'Echoes In The Night' LP. Eric plays on the title track.

OCTOBER 1985

1

Starts tour of Japan.

14

Anchorage, Alaska.

20

Civic Hall, Guildford. Phil Collins joins Eric's band for 'Layla', 'Knock On Wood' and 'You Don't Know Like I Know', and to conclude the evening Carl Perkins joins the line-up for 'Matchbox', 'Blue Suede Shoes' and 'Goodnight Irene'.

21

Limehouse Studios, London. Eric, George Harrison, Ringo Starr, Dave Edumunds, Earl Slick, Rosanne Cash and others take part in the filming of a TV Special on Carl Perkins which is to be broadcast on Channel 4 TV on New Year's Day 1986. Among the songs they perform are 'Matchbox', 'Blue Suede Shoes', 'Blue Moon Of Kentucky', 'That's All Right' and 'Whole Lotta' Shakin' Goin' On'.

23

Lausanne, Switzerland.

24

Zurich. Followed by ten dates in Italy.

NOVEMBER 1985

4

'Edge Of Darkness', 6 part BBC2 thriller serial, is broadcast. Eric performs title music.

DECEMBER 1985

3

Dingwalls, Camden Town. Eric joins Buddy Guy and Junior Wells for 40-minute instrumental jam session.

6

Eric joins Sting on stage at Milan's Teatro Tenda to perform 'Devil And The Deep Blue Sea'.

12

Eric peforms with The End Of The Pier Restoration Band at The Dickens pub in Southend. Their two and a half hour set is comprised of rock'n'roll classics, and the band also include Gary Brooker and Henry Spinetti.

19, 22

Eric performs four numbers – 'Two Young Lovers', 'Cocaine', 'Solid Rock' and 'Further On Up The Road' – with Dire Straits at Hammersmith Odeon, London.

Left: With Phil Collins at Guildford Civic Hall, October 20, 1985. (Stuart Pearsall)

And an echo of showbusiness greats from the past

Stars shine for a rock 'n' roll giant

Carl Perkins (centre), Clapton, left, and Harrison. Front: Ringo and Dave Edmunds
Picture: TERRY O'NEILL

SOME of Britain's top rock stars played their hearts out yesterday for their boyhood hero.

Guitarists Eric Clapton and Dave Edmunds and ex-Beatles George Harrison and Ringo Starr were among the musicians who gathered to honour 53-year-old rock 'n' roll singer Carl Perkins.

They joined him on stage to perform some of his Fifties hits, including Blue Suede Shoes, which became rock music classics.

The two former Beatles, it was a moment to savour. Much of their work in the early Sixties had been influenced by Perkins. Harrison, together with John Lennon and Paul McCartney, used to examine his songs in minute detail to copy his distinctive sound.

Yesterday's session, filmed in London by Channel 4 for screening in the New Year, came about after Perkins contacted the musicians, asking them to help him produce the 'best rock 'n' roll spectacle the world's ever seen.'

Far left: Eric on stage during the Philadelphia Live Aid concert, July 1985. (Ken Regan/LFI)

Left: At the Montreux Jazz Festival, 1986, with Luther Alison and Otis Rush. (Marc Roberty)

Bottom left: With the Stones at London's 100 Club. (Marc Roberty)

FEBRUARY 1986
23

Jams with Rolling Stones at 100 Club in London's Oxford Street alongside Pete Townshend and Jeff Beck.

25

Presents Rolling Stones with their 'Lifetime Achievement' Award at the Grammy Awards live from the Roof Gardens Club in Kensington which is relayed by satellite to Los Angeles.

MARCH 1986

Paul Brady releases his 'Back To The Centre' album. Eric plays on 'Deep In Your Heart'.

APRIL 1986
6

Eric appears in sketch at *Comedy Aid* and sings in the chorus during 'Feed The World' with Bob Geldof and Midge Ure.

8

Short interview on Radio One.

Most of April and May is spent recording 'August' at Sunset Sound in Los Angeles.

Tracks recorded include 'Miss You', 'Tearing Us Apart', 'Lady From Verona', 'Behind The Mask', 'Run', 'Bad Influence', 'Walk Away', 'Hung Up On Your Love', 'Take A Chance', 'Hold On', 'Walking The White Line', 'Holy Mother' and 'Grand Illusion'.

The sessions are produced by Phil Collins who also plays drums. Tina Turner guests on 'Tearing Us Apart' and 'Hold On'. The rest of the band are Greg Phillinganes on keyboards and backing vocals and Nathan East on bass.

JUNE 1986
20

Eric appears at the Prince's Trust 10th Birthday Party concert at Wembley Arena alongside Midge Ure, Mark King, Phil Collins, Mark Knopfler, Elton John, Rod Stewart, Mick Jagger, David Bowie, Tina Turner, Sting, Howard Jones, Joan Armatrading, Paul McCartney, Bryan Adams, Francis Rossi, Rick Parfitt, Paul Young, George Michael and John Illsley.

The show is filmed and recorded for later release. Bowie and Jagger's version of 'Dancing In The Street' is the only song not released from this concert.

28

Rehearsals start for upcoming tour. Band now consists of Phil Collins on drums, Nathan East on bass and Greg Phillinganes on keyboards.

JULY 1986
3

Isle Of Calf Festival, Oslo, Norway.

1986

4

Roskilde Festival, Copenhagen, Denmark.

9

Jazz Festival, Montreux, Switzerland.

On the eve of his own performance Eric jams with Otis Rush alongside Luther Alison. Complete show broadcast on Swiss radio.

10

Jazz Festival, Montreux, Switzerland.

Robert Cray jams with Eric on 'Ramblin' On My Mind' and 'Have You Ever Loved A Woman'. The show is filmed and recorded.

12

Juan Les Pins Festival, Antibes, France.

14, 15

NEC, Birmingham, England.

Both shows are recorded; 15th is filmed. Robert Cray jams on 'Further On Up The Road' on 15th.

Basic set for tour is 'Crossroads', 'White Room', 'I Shot The Sheriff', 'Wanna Make Love To You', 'Run', 'Miss You', 'Same Old Blues', 'Tearing Us Apart', 'Holy Mother', 'Behind The Mask', 'Badge', 'Let It Rain', 'In The Air Tonight', 'Cocaine', 'Layla', 'Sunshine Of Your Love', 'Further On Up The Road'.

17

Capital Radio, London, broadcast Eric Clapton interview.

AUGUST 1986

11

Lionel Richie releases 'Dancing On

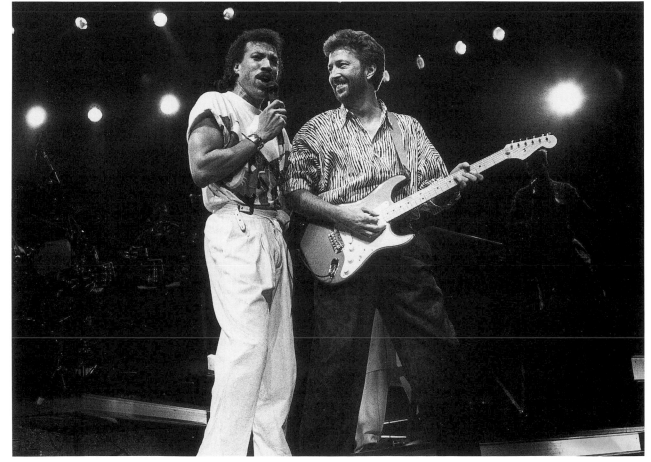

Right: With Lionel Richie at New York's Madison Square Garden. (Chuck Pulin/Starfile)

Left: (Pictorial Press)

Bottom left: Eric walks out to bat on Ripley Village Green. (Pictorial Press)

Wood on bass and Henry Spinetti on drums. They record three takes of 'The Usual', one of 'Song With No Name', seven of 'Had A Dream About You', three of 'Five And Dimmer' and one of 'To Fall In Love'.

29

Leona Boyd releases her 'Persona' LP. Eric plays on 'Labyrinth'.

SEPTEMBER 1986

Eric records two tracks for the soundtrack of *Colour Of Money*: 'It's In the Way That You Use It' which appears on the 'August' LP and 'It's My Life Baby' on which he is backed by the Big Town Playboys but which remains unreleased.

OCTOBER 1986
16

Fox Theater, St. Louis, Mo.
    Eric plays at Chuck Berry's two 60th Birthday Party concerts, singing and playing on 'Wee Wee Hours'. The concerts are filmed and recorded for later release.

Eric Clapton: **Chuck appeared and he sat down next to me on a couch and said, "Hi, I'm Chuck Berry, you're Eric Clapton. Nice to meet you." Then he said, "Hang on a second" and shouted, "Bring the camera in." Then he started to interview me about him!**

27

Madison Square Garden, New York.
    Joins Lionel Richie for 'Tonight Will Be Alright'.

29

Eric plays 'Miss You', 'It's In the Way That You Use It' and 'I Shot The Sheriff' with house band on *Nightlife*.

NOVEMBER 1986
8

Eric joins Robert Cray at London's Mean Fiddler for 'Smoking Gun', 'Playing In The Dirt', 'The Last

The Ceiling' LP. Eric plays on 'Tonight Will Be Alright'.

14

Eric jams with Prince at The Gardens nightclub, Kensington, on a few Al Green numbers.

Eric Clapton: **Oh, that was great. He played 'Can't Get Next To You', an old Al Green song, for about half an hour. Prince saw me and invited me up.**

15

Charity cricket match at Finchley Cricket Club. Eric jams with Chicken Shack during the post-match party.

16

Eric and band film video for 'Tearing Us Apart' at Ronnie Scott's Club in London's Soho. An invitation only audience is treated to several versions of this track and various instrumental jams including Prince's '1999'.

21

EC attends Bob Geldof's stag party at Groucho's in Soho.

27, 28

Records with Bob Dylan at London's Townhouse Studios in Shepherds Bush, with Ronnie

1986

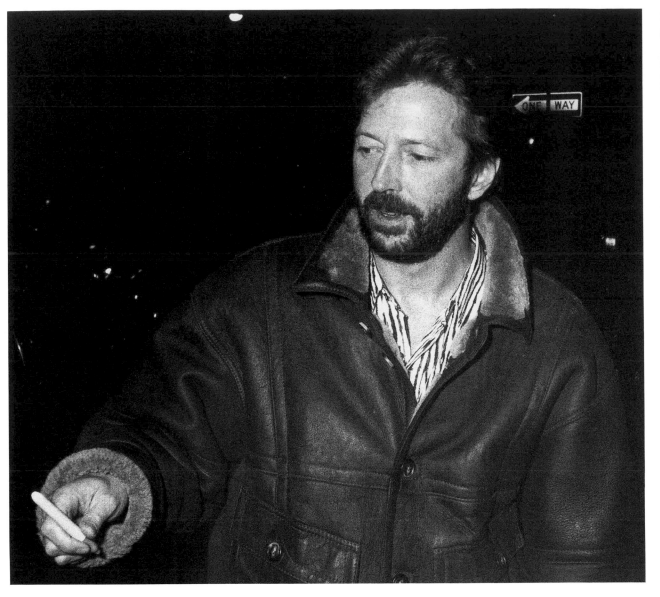

AUGUST
UK Duck Records WX71 925 476-1
US Duck Records 25476
Released November 1986

Side One:
1. It's In The Way That You Use It
2. Run
3. Tearing Us Apart
4. Bad Influence
5. Walk Away
6. Hung Up On Your Love
Side Two:
7. Take A Chance
8. Hold On
9. Miss You
10. Holy Mother
11. Behind The Mask

Above: (Vinni Zuffante/Starfile)

Below: (Chuck Pulin/Starfile)

Far right, above: With Roomful Of Blues guitarist Ronnie Earl. (Steve Weitzman/Starfile)

Far right, below: With Keith Richards at the Ritz Club, New York, November 1986. (Gene Shaw/Starfile)

Time', 'Bad Influence' and 'Phone Booth'. The final song was released as a free flexi-disc with the May issue of *Guitar Player* magazine.

Eric Clapton: It's a lovely band to play with. It's easy to slot in with someone like that because all the songs he writes are so natural and still loosely within a blues framework.

20, 21
The Metro, Boston. Opening of short club tour.

23, 24
The Ritz, New York.
   Keith Richards joins Eric for 'Cocaine' and 'Layla' on 23.
   'August' LP released on the 24th.

Bob Geldof releases his first solo album 'Deep In The Heart Of Nowhere'. EC plays on 'Love Like A Rocket', 'August Was A Heavy Month', 'The Beat Of The Night' and 'Good Boys In The Wrong'.

DECEMBER 1986 8-16
Records *Lethal Weapon* soundtrack at Townhouse Studios in London's Shepherds Bush.

23
Dunsfold Village Hall. Plays with Gary Brooker in charity show.

25
Eric's Birmingham NEC show from July 15 is broadcast on British TV.

1987

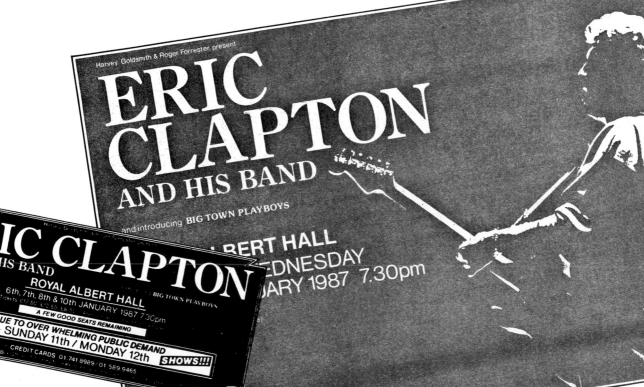

The year starts with a UK and European tour.

JANUARY 1987
3, 4
Apollo, Manchester.

5
'Behind The Mask' single released.

6, 7, 8
Royal Albert Hall, London.
Sting and Steve Winwood join Eric for 'Money For Nothing' and 'Sunshine Of Your Love' on 8th.

10, 11, 12
Royal Albert Hall, London.
Phil Collins joins Eric for the last two shows on 11th and 12th. All three shows are recorded but remain unreleased.

16
Ahoy Halle, Rotterdam, Holland.

17
Forest National, Brussels, Belgium.

18
Le Zenith, Paris, France.

20
Westfalenhalle, Dortmund, West Germany.

21
Sporthalle, Hamburg, West Germany.

22
Festhalle, Frankfurt, West Germany.

23
Olympiahalle, Munich, West Germany.

26
Palatrussardi, Milan, Italy.

29
Palaeur, Rome, Italy.

30
Palasport, Florence, Italy.
The band for this tour comprised Mark Knopfler on guitar, Greg Phillinganes on keyboards, Nathan East on bass and Steve Ferrone on drums. Mark played on all British dates as well as Brussels and Paris.
The set was 'Crossroads', 'White Room', 'I Shot The Sheriff', 'Hung Up On Your Love', 'Wonderful Tonight', 'Miss You', 'Same Old Blues', 'Tearing Us Apart', 'Holy Mother', 'Badge', 'Let It Rain', 'Cocaine', 'Layla', 'Money For Nothing', and 'Sunshine Of Your Love'.

FEBRUARY 1987
9
Eric receives BPI Award at Grosvenor House Hotel in London. The event is broadcast live on BBC1.

14
Bob Geldof and Eric perform 'Love Like A Rocket' on *Saturday Superstore*.

15, 16
EC records three tracks with Jack Bruce, two of which are eventually released on 'Willpower'.

19
Eric performs 'Behind The Mask' on *Top Of The Pops*.

MARCH 1987
2
Tina Turner releases 'What You See is What You Get' as a 12-inch single. Eric is credited as playing guitar.

23
'It's the Way That You Use It' single released.

25
Attends Elton John's 40th birthday party.

27
Eric plays charity gig at Cranleigh Golf Club in Surrey. Numbers played include 'Tulsa Time', 'Behind The Mask', 'Walkin' The Dog', 'Route 66', 'Crossroads', 'Lay Down Sally', 'Black Magic Woman', 'The Bear', 'Alberta', 'Tearing Us Apart', 'Knock On Wood', 'Ramblin' On My Mind', 'Red Dress', 'Boogie', 'Walkin' On Sunset', 'Sunshine Of Your Love', 'Baby's Gone And Left Me', 'Cocaine;' and 'Further On Up The Road'.

APRIL 1987
11
Oakland Coliseum, Oakland, Ca. Start of US tour.

13
Pacific Amphitheater, Costa Mesa, Ca.

14
The Forum, Los Angeles, Ca.

1987

15

Ebony Showcase Theater, Los
Angeles, Ca.
  B.B. King special filmed here
with Eric, Phil Collins, Chaka Khan,
Gladys Knight, Paul Butterfield, Dr
John, Stevie Ray Vaughn, Albert
King, Billy Ocean and Etta James.

16

McNichols Arena, Denver, Co.

18

Civic Centre, St Paul, Minn.

19

Rosemont Horizon, Chicago, Ill.
  After the show Eric, Phil Collins
and Robert Cray head down to the
Limelight Club for a 70-minute jam
with Buddy Guy.

21

Market Square Arena, Indianapolis,
Ind.

22

Joe Louis Arena, Detroit, Mich.

23

Richfield Coliseum, Cleveland,
Ohio.

25

Capitol Centre, Largo, Md.

26

Civic Centre, Providence, RI. This
show is recorded but remains
unreleased.

27

Madison Square Garden, New
York. This show is recorded but
remains unreleased.
  The band for this US tour
comprised Phil Collins on drums,
Greg Phillinganes on keyboards and
Nathan East on bass. The set
consisted of 'Crossroads', 'White
Room', 'I Shot The Sheriff', 'Hung
Up On Your Love', 'Wonderful
Tonight', 'Miss You', 'Same Old
Blues', 'Tearing Us Apart', 'Holy
Mother', 'Badge', 'Let It Rain',
'Cocaine', 'Layla', 'Further On Up
The Road', 'Sunshine Of Your
Love'.
  As Robert Cray was the
support artist for the tour he ended
up jamming most nights on 'Further
On Up The Road'.

MAY 1987
6

Eric joins Lionel Richie at Wembley
Arena for 'Tonight Will Be Alright'
and 'Brickhouse'.

JUNE 1987
1, 2, 3, 4

Rehearsals at Brixton Academy for
the upcoming Prince's Trust
concerts.

5, 6

Wembley Arena, London.
  Prince's Trust shows where
Eric performed alongside Mark
King, Midge Ure, Bryan Adams,

Left: At the Prince's Trust Concert, Wembley Arena, 1987. Eric on stage with, amongst others, George Harrison, Ringo Starr and Jeff Lynne. (Vinnie Zuffante/ Starfile)

Phil Collins, Ben E. King, Spandau Ballet, George Harrison and Ringo Starr.

The highlight is an emotional version of 'While My Guitar Gently Weeps' which features some great interplay between George and Eric.

The show on the 6th is filmed and recorded for later release.

8

'Tearing Us Apart' single released.

John Astley releases his 'Everyone Loves The Pilot' LP. Eric plays on 'Jane's Getting Serious'.

18

EC joins Tina Turner at Wembley for 'Tearing Us Apart'. The show is recorded and later broadcast on Radio One and released on album.

JULY 1987
4

Eric plays at Island Records 25th Birthday Party at Pinewood Studios, performing 'I Shot The Sheriff' with The Island All Stars. He later jams with Andy Summers, John Martyn and Ringo Starr.

11

Star of six part Radio One series on Eric called *Behind The Mask – The Story Of Eric Clapton.*

AUGUST 1987
10

Prince's Trust concert released on album.

FINCHLEY CRICKET CLUB

David Gower / Clive Radley
Benefit Match

Friday 14th August 1987

ADMISSION FOR EVENING
ENTERTAINMENT ONLY
£5.00

Right of Admission reserved

14

Eric plays in charity cricket match at Finchley Cricket Club and in the evening performs a 90-minute set with Stan Webb's Chicken Shack. Numbers performed include 'The Thrill Is Gone', 'I'd Rather Go Blind', 'Sweet Sixteen', 'Further On Up The Road', 'Every Day I Have The Blues' and 'Cocaine'.

SEPTEMBER 1987
4

Eric jams with Roomful Of Blues at the Lonestar Café in New York. The same afternoon he'd filmed the 'After Midnight' promo advert for a beer company at the club.

Eric Clapton: **Fantastic band. Ronnie Earl is a great player. They played their whole set then I got up and jammed with them. Phenomenal!**

14

'Cream Of Eric Clapton' released.

OCTOBER 1987
6

Eric and Buddy Guy perform at Ronnie Scott's Club in Soho. Their set is filmed for inclusion on a *South Bank Show* TV special.

Eric Clapton: **They showed some of it on TV, late hours. I watched some of that and I was very disappointed with the sound mix because you can hardly hear Buddy.**

7

Bob Dylan's 'The Usual' single, on which Eric guests, is released.

9

Buddy Guy plays the last of his two show at Dingwalls in Camden Lock. Eric joins him for the final two-hour show. Among the highlights were 'Stormy Monday', 'Sweet Sixteen', 'My Time After A While' and 'The Things I Used To Do'.

12

Sting releases his 'Nothing Like The Sun' album. Eric plays acoustic guitar on 'They Dance Alone'.

19

Hearts Of Fire soundtrack released. Eric plays on 'The Usual', 'Night After Night' and 'I Had A Dream About You'.

23

Entertainment Centre, Sydney, Australia. Start of Australian and Japanese tour.

24

Entertainment Centre, Brisbane, Australia.

27

Sports and Entertainment Centre, Melbourne, Australia.

NOVEMBER 1987
2, 4, 5

Budokan, Tokyo, Japan.

7

Nagoya Gym, Nagoya, Japan.

9

Castle Hall, Osaka, Japan.

The band for these dates comprised Steve Ferrone on drums, Alan Clark on keyboards and Nathan East on bass.

George Harrison releases his 'Cloud 9' LP. Eric plays on 'Cloud 9', 'That's What It Takes', 'Devil's Radio' and 'Wreck Óf The Hesperus'.

DECEMBER 1987
6

South Bank Show TV documentary on Eric is broadcast in the UK. The programme includes interviews with Eric, his mother and grandmother and also has rare footage from the unreleased *Rolling Hotel* film which documented his 1978 European tour.

19

Joins Gary Brooker, Henry Spinetti and Andy Fairweather-Low at Dunsfold Village Hall.

Far left: (David Seelig/Starfile)

Far left, inset: Eric shelters from the rain with, amongst others, Ian Botham and Bill Wyman. (Petra Zeig/Starfile)

Left: With Buddy Guy at Ronnie Scotts Club, London. (Marc Roberty)

Left, bottom: (Marc Roberty)

THE CREAM OF ERIC CLAPTON
UK Polydor ECTV1
No US release
Released September 1987

Side One:
1. Layla
2. Badge
3. I Feel Free
4. Sunshine Of Your Love
5. Strange Brew
6. White Room
7. Cocaine
8. I Shot The Sheriff
Side Two:
9. Behind The Mask
10. Forever Man
11. Lay Down Sally
12. Knockin' On Heaven's Door
13. Wonderful Tonight
14. Let It Grow
15. Promises
16. I've Got A Rock'n'Roll Heart

1988

CROSSROADS
UK Polydor 835 261-1
US Polygram 835261-1
Released April 1988

Record One Side One:
1. Boom Boom
2. Honey In Your Hips
3. Baby What's Wrong
4. I Wish You Would
5. A Certain Girl
6. Good Morning Little Schoolgirl
7. I Ain't Got You
8. For Your Love
9. Got To Hurry
Side Two:
10. Lonely Years
11. Bernard Jenkins
12. Hideaway
13. All Your Love
14. Ramblin' On My Mind
15. Have You Ever Loved A Woman
Record Two Side One:
16. Wrapping Paper
17. I Feel Free
18. Spoonful
19. Lawdy Mama
20. Strange Brew
21. Sunshine Of Your Love
22. Tales Of Brave Ulysses
23. Steppin' Out
Side Two:
24. Anyone For Tennis
25. White Room
26. Crossroads
27. Badge
28. Presence Of The Lord
29. Can't Find My Way Home
30. Sleeping In The Ground
Record Three Side One:
31. Comin' Home
32. Blues Power
33. After Midnight
34. Let It Rain
35. Tell The Truth
36. Roll It Over
Side Two:
37. Layla

JANUARY 1988
22, 23
NEC, Birmingham. Start of UK tour.

Band comprised Steve Ferrone on drums, Nathan East on bass, Alan Clark on keyboards, Ray Cooper on percussion, Mark Knopfler on guitar, and Katie Kissoon and Tessa Niles on backing vocals.

25, 26, 27, 29, 30, 31
Royal Albert Hall, London.

FEBRUARY 1988
2, 3, 4
Royal Albert Hall, London.

7
Civic Hall, Guildford. Elton John and Phil Collins join the band for various songs.

The set for this tour was 'Crossroads', 'White Room', 'I Shot The Sheriff', 'Wonderful Tonight', 'Run', 'Same Old Blues', 'Tearing Us Apart', 'Holy Mother', 'Badge', 'Let It Rain', 'Cocaine', 'Layla', 'Behind The Mask', 'Sunshine Of Your Love', 'Money For Nothing', 'Further On Up The Road'.

8
Eric attends the BPI awards at London's Royal Albert Hall where The Who perform.

MARCH 1988
25
Eric records 'The Robbery' at Townhouse Studios in London for the soundtrack of *Buster*.

Eric Clapton: I just played some guitar. It was part of the score for the robbery scene which is quite early on in the film.

31
Tina Turner releases her 'Live In Europe' double album. Eric plays on 'Tearing Us Apart'.

APRIL 1988
18
'Crossroads' retrospective released, containing many unreleased gems.

23, 24, 27, 28, 29
Eric records the soundtrack to *Homeboy* at Townhouse Studios in London.

MAY 1988
7, 8, 14, 15, 21
Eric records the soundtrack to *Peace In Our Time* at Townhouse Studios.

30, 31
Rehearsals with Dire Straits at Brixton Academy.

JUNE 1988
1, 2, 3
Rehearsals with Dire Straits at Brixton Academy.

4

Rehearsals for Prince's Trust.

5, 6

Royal Albert Hall, London.

Eric plays at these two Prince's Trust shows with Steve Ferrone on drums, Nathan East on bass, Mark Knopfler on guitar, Elton John on keyboards, Phil Collins on drums, and Katie Kissoon and Tessa Niles on backing vocals.

The set comprised 'Behind The Mask', 'Cocaine', 'Money For Nothing', 'I Don't Wanna Go On With You Like That' and 'Layla'. The concert concluded with all the evening's performers, including Phil Collins, Joe Cocker, Peter Gabriel, Howard Jones, The Bee Gees, Midge Ure, Wet Wet Wet and T'Pau, joining in on 'With A Little Help From My Friends'.

7

Rehearsals with Dire Straits at Brixton Academy.

8, 9

Eric plays with Dire Straits at two warm up shows at London's Hammersmith Odeon.

11

Eric joins Dire Straits at the *Free Nelson Mandela* concert at Wembley Stadium which is televised worldwide.

15-25

Eric records with Davina McCall.

23

This year's Prince's Trust show broadcast on TV.

JULY 1988
2

Charity show at Wintershall, Surrey, with Gary Brooker on keyboards and vocals, Phil Collins on drums and vocals, Andy

Far left, top: (Vinnie Zuffante/ Starfile)

Far left, bottom: (George Chin/ Starfile)

This page: With Dire Straits at the Nelson Mandela concert, Wembley Stadium 1988. (Vinnie Zuffante/Starfile)

38. Mean Old World
39. Key To The Highway
40. Crossroads
Record Four Side One:
41. Got To Get Better In A Little While
42. Evil
43. One More Chance
44. Mean Old Frisco
45. Snake Lake Blues
Side Two:
46. Let It Grow
47. Ain't That Lovin' You
48. Motherless Children
49. I Shot The Sheriff
50. Better Make It Through Today
Record Five Side One:
51. The Sky Is Crying
52. I Found A Love
53. (When Things Go Wrong) It Hurts Me Too
54. Whatcha Gonna Do
55. Knockin' On Heaven's Door
56. Someone Like You
Side Two:
57. Hello Old Friend
58. Sign Language
59. Further On Up The Road
60. Lay Down Sally
61. Wonderful Tonight
Record Six Side One:
62. Cocaine
63. Promises
64. If I Don't Be There By Morning
65. Double Trouble
66. I Can't Stand It
67. The Shape You're In
Side Two:
68. Heaven Is One Step Away
69. She's Waiting
70. Too Bad
71. Miss You
72. Wanna Make Love To You
73. After Midnight

1988

Right: With Phil Collins, Rich Wills and Mike Rutherford, Wintershall, July 1988. (Marc Roberty)

Right, below: (Marc Roberty)

Fairweather-Low on guitar and vocals, Howard Jones on keyboards, Mike Rutherford on guitar, Henry Spinetti on drums, Jody Linscott on percussion, Rick Wills on bass, Frank Mead and Mel Collins on saxes, and Vicky and Sam Brown on backing vocals.

Among the songs in their two-and-a-half-hour set were 'You Can't Hurry Love', 'Abacab', 'Wide Eyed And Legless', 'No One Is To Blame', 'Behind The Mask', 'It's In The Way That You Use It', 'Cocaine' and 'Whiter Shade Of Pale'.

4
'After Midnight' single released.

AUGUST 1988
Buckwheat Zydeco releases his 'Taking It Home' LP. Eric plays on 'Why Does Love Got To Be So Sad'.

Eric Clapton: He wasn't there when I did it. That came about through a mutual friend called Rob Fabroni who produced 'No Reason To Cry'. When Rob came to

England earlier this year he brought the tape with him. I played on the thing . . . two takes.

22-31
Rehearsals for upcoming US and Canadian tour in Dallas. Band comprises Alan Clark on keyboards, Jody Linscott on percussion, Mark Knopfler on guitar, Steve Ferrone on drums, Nathan East on bass and Katie Kissoon and Tessa Niles on backing vocals.

SEPTEMBER 1988
1
Starplex Amphitheater, Dallas, Tx.

2
Lakefront Arena, New Orleans, Lo.

4
Civic Arena, Pittsburgh, Penn.

6
Meadowlands Arena, Rutherford, N.J.

7
Spectrum, Philadelphia, Penn.

8
Capitol Centre, Largo, Md.

10
Civic Centre, Hartford, Conn.

11
Nassau Coliseum, Uniondale, N.Y.

13, 14
Great Woods, Boston, Mass.

16
Palace, Detroit, Mich.

17
Alpine Valley, Milwaukee, Wi.

19
Fiddler's Green, Denver, Co.

21
Shoreline Amphitheater, San Francisco, Ca.

22
Arco Arena, Sacramento, Ca.

23
Irvine Meadows Amphitheater, Lugana Hills, Ca.

25
Hollywood Bowl, Los Angeles, Ca.

This page: (Vinnie Zuffante)

Eric joins Elton John for 'Saturday Night's Alright For Fighting'.

26
Coliseum, Portland, Or.

27
The Dome, Tacoma, Wa.

28
PNE Coliseum, Vancouver, B.C.

29
Pantages Theater, Los Angeles, Ca. Joins Little Feat for 'Apolitical Blues'.

Right: (Gene Shaw/Starfile)

Right, below: (David Seelig/Starfile)

30
Olympic Saddledome, Calgary, Alberta.

OCTOBER 1988
1
Saskatchewan Place, Saskatoon, Saskatchewan.

3
The Arena, Winnipeg, Manitoba.

4
MET Centre, Minneapolis, Minn.

6
Forum, Montreal, Quebec.

7
Maple Leaf Gardens, Toronto, Ontario.

8
Copps Coliseum, Hamilton, Ontario. Eric joined his support band Buckwheat Zydeco for 'Why Does Love Got To Be So Bad'.

The set throughout the US and Canadian tour consisted of 'Crossroads', 'White Room', 'I Shot The Sheriff', 'Lay Down Sally', 'Wonderful Tonight', 'Tearing Us Apart', 'After Midnight', 'Can't Find My Way Home', 'Motherless Children', 'Same Old Blues', 'Cocaine', 'Layla', 'Money For Nothing', 'Sunshine Of Your Love'.

10
Gail Anne Dorsey releases her 'The Corporate World' LP. Eric plays on 'Wasted County'.

11
Eric jams with Jack Bruce at New York's Bottom Line Club on 'Spoonful' and 'Sunshine Of Your Love'.

26-29
Rehearsals in Tokyo for Japanese tour.

31
Rainbow Hall, Nagoya, Japan.

NOVEMBER 1988
2
The Dome, Tokyo, Japan.
This show is filmed for subsequent broadcast on Japanese TV and radio.

4
Budokan, Tokyo, Japan.

Sting joins Eric's band for 'Money For Nothing'.

5

The Stadium, Osaka, Japan.

The band for Japan comprised Mark Knopfler on guitar, Elton John on keyboards and vocals, Steve Ferrone on drums, Ray Cooper on percussion, Nathan East on bass, Alan Clark on keyboards, and Katie Kissoon and Tessa Niles on backing vocals.

The set consisted of 'Crossroads', 'White Room', 'I Shot The Sheriff', 'Lay Down Sally', 'Wonderful Tonight', 'Tearing Us Apart', 'Can't Find My Way Home', 'After Midnight', 'Money For Nothing', 'Candle In The Wind', 'I Guess That's Why They Call It The Blues', 'I Don't Wanna Go On With You Like That', 'I'm Still Standing', 'Daniel', 'Cocaine', 'Layla', 'Solid Rock', 'Saturday Night's Alright For Fighting' and 'Sunshine Of Your Love'.

November also saw the release of the 'One Moment In Time' LP. Eric plays on The Bunbury's 'Fight' alongside The Bee Gees on backing vocals, Laurence Cottle on bass, Duncan Makay on keyboards, and David English and Ian Botham on additional vocals.

28

Hard Rock Café, London.

Eric plays with Jeff Beck, backed by Mitch Mitchell on drums and Noel Redding on bass following a charity auction for the Celia Hammond Trust.

DECEMBER 1988

Jim Capaldi releases his 'Some Come Running' LP. Eric plays on 'You Are The One' and 'Oh Lord Why Lord' which also features George Harrison.

Eric Clapton: I played on two tracks. I played on more but I think two tracks are going to be used. It's a very good sounding record.

23

Dunsfold Village Hall, Surrey.

Eric plays with Gary Brooker, Andy Fairweather-Low, Henry Spinetti and Frank Mead.

Top, left to right: Mick Jones, Gene Cornish, Carole King, EC and Nathan East at New York's China Club, December 1988. (Dominick Conde/Starfile)

Below: Mark Knopfler. (Bob Gruen/Starfile)

1989

Also on the 25th Eric appears on the *Wogan* show on TV.

The set for the above UK dates was 'Crossroads', 'White Room', 'I Shot The Sheriff', 'Bell Bottom Blues', 'After Midnight', 'Wonderful Tonight', 'Can't Find My Way Home', 'Forever Man', 'Same Old

JANUARY 1989
10

Eric jams with Womack and Womack at Dingwalls in Camden Lock.

16

Sheffield City Hall. Start of UK tour.

The band consists of Phil Collins on drums, Nathan East on bass and Greg Phillinganes on keyboards.

17

City Hall, Newcastle-on-Tyne.

18

Playhouse, Edinburgh.

20, 21, 22, 24, 25, 26

Royal Albert Hall, London.

Blues', 'Knockin' On Heaven's Door', 'Easy Lover', 'Tearing Us Apart', 'Cocaine', 'Layla', 'Behind The Mask', 'Sunshine Of Your Love'.

28, 29, 30

Royal Albert Hall, London.

FEBRUARY 1989
1, 2, 3

Royal Albert Hall, London.

For the final six shows at the Albert Hall Eric's band comprised Mark Knopfler on guitar, Steve Ferrone on drums, Nathan East on

---

EXTRA SHOWS BY PHENOMENAL DEMAND!

HARVEY GOLDSMITH ENTS BY ARRANGEMENT WITH ROGER FORRESTER presents

ERIC CLAPTON
AND HIS BAND
PLUS SPECIAL GUESTS

~~...TH JAN~~ SOLD OUT
~~SATUR...21st JAN~~ SOLD OUT
~~SUNDAY...nd JAN~~ SOLD OUT
~~TUESDA...th JAN~~ SOLD OUT
~~WEDNES...25th JAN~~
~~THURS...6th JAN~~ SOLD OUT
SATURDAY 28th JAN
SUNDAY 29th JAN
MONDAY 30th JAN
WEDNESDAY 1st FEB
THURSDAY 2nd FEB
FRIDAY 3rd FEB

TICKETS FROM £11.00
FROM BOX OFFICE 01-589-8212 & USUAL AGENTS.
CREDIT CARD HOTLINES:
748-1414. 240-7200. 818-6131
(subject to booking fee)

Royal Albert Hall

1989

bass, Greg Phillinganes and Alan Clark on keyboards, Ray Cooper on percussion, and Katie Kissoon and Tessa Niles on backing vocals.

The set for these shows consisted of 'Crossroads', 'White Room', 'I Shot The Sheriff', 'Bell Bottom Blues', 'Lay Down Sally', 'Wonderful Tonight', 'Wanna Make Love To You', 'After Midnight', 'Can't Find My Way Home', 'Forever Man', 'Same Old Blues', 'Tearing Us Apart', 'Cocaine', 'Layla', 'Solid Rock' (Feb 1, 2 and 3 only), 'Behind The Mask', 'Sunshine Of Your Love'.

7

Eric records title music for the James Bond film *Licence To Kill* which remains unreleased due to legal problems.

MARCH 1989

Eric spends most of March and April at New York's Power Station and Skyline studios for the recording of 'Journeyman' and 'Lethal Weapon Two'. Tracks recorded include 'No Alibis', 'Old Love', 'Hound Dog', 'Before You Accuse Me', 'Pretending', 'Breaking Point', 'Higher Power', 'Hard Times', 'Lead Me On',

Top: EC with Ozzie Osbourne and Grace Jones. (Bob Gruen/ Starfile)

Centre: With Bill Wyman. (Pictorial Press)

Bottom: Carl Perkins and EC at New York's Bottom Line. (Chuck Pulin/Starfile)

'Something About You', 'Running On Faith' (two versions – one with electric guitar solo and one with dobro), 'Murdoch's Men', 'Anything For Your Love', 'Run So Far', 'Forever', 'Don't Turn Your Back'.

APRIL 1989
3

Carole King releases her 'City Streets' album. Eric plays on 'City Streets' and 'Ain't That The Way'.

MAY 1989

Eric is back in New York for final overdubs and mixing of 'Journeyman'.

9

Eric jams with Carl Perkins at New

York's Bottom Line Club, and plays on 'Mean Woman Blues', 'Matchbox', 'Roll Over Beethoven', 'Maybelline', 'Whole Lotta Shakin'', 'Hound Dog', 'Blue Suede Shoes' and 'Goin' Down The Road Feeling Bad'.

31

Eric attends the Elvis Awards ceremony at New York's Armoury and jams on an all-star finale of 'I

Hear You Knockin'' alongside Keith Richards, Jeff Healey, Tina Turner, Clarence Clemons, Vernon Reid, Dave Edmunds and others.

Eric receives an Elvis Award for best guitarist which is presented to him by Keith Richards.

JUNE 1989
5

Eric attends the reception following Bill Wyman's marriage to Mandy Smith along with various members of The Rolling Stones.

JULY 1989

1

Eric plays with Band Du Lac at a charity concert at Wintershall, Surrey.

The band consists of Gary Brooker on keyboards and vocals, Dave Bronze on bass, Henry Spinetti and Phil Collins on drums, Frank Mead and Mel Collins on saxes, Sam and Vicki Brown on vocals, Andy Fairweather-Low and Mike Rutherford on guitars and Steve Winwood on keyboards.

The two-and-a-half-hour set includes 'Pick Up The Pieces', 'Ain't That Peculiar', 'Can I Get A Witness', 'Freedom Overspill', 'Lead Me To The Water', 'All I Need Is A Miracle', 'Old Love', 'Stop In The Name Of Love', 'You Don't Know Like I Know', 'Respect', 'Throwing It All Away', 'A Bridge Across The River', 'Lay Down Sally', 'Souvenir Of London', 'Roll With It', 'STOP', 'Loco In Acapulco', 'Gin House', 'Cocaine', 'Whiter Shade Of Pale', 'You Can't Hurry Love', 'Night And Day' and 'Gimme Some Lovin''.

6, 7

Statenhal, The Hague, Holland.
Start of European, Middle Eastern and African tour. Band consists of Steve Ferrone on drums, Nathan East on bass, Phil Palmer on guitar, Alan Clark on keyboards, Ray Cooper on percussion, and Katie Kissoon and Tessa Niles on backing vocals.

9, 10

Hallenstadion, Zurich, Switzerland.

13

Sultan's Pool, Jerusalem, Israel.

14

Zemach Amphitheatre, Sea Of Galilee, Israel.

15, 17

Caesarea Amphitheatre, Caesarea, Palestine.

22

Somhlolo National Stadium, Swaziland.

25, 26

Conference Centre, Harare, Zimbabwe.

28

Boipuso Hall, Gaborone, Botswana.

30

Machava National Stadium, Maputo, Mozambique.

This amazing concert was attended by 102,000 people who paid £1.00 a head. All proceeds were given to a local housing project. The concert was filmed.

The set for this tour was 'Crossroads', 'White Room', 'I Shot The Sheriff', 'Bell Bottom Blues', 'Lay Down Sally', 'Wonderful Tonight', 'I Wanna Make Love To You', 'After Midnight', 'Can't Find My Way Home', 'Forever Man', 'Same Old Blues', 'Tearing Us Apart', 'Cocaine', 'Layla', 'Badge', 'Sunshine Of Your Love'.

Top: (C. Basiliano)

Inset: (John Peek)

Centre: With Keith Richards at the Elvis Awards. (Bob Gruen/Starfile)

Bottom: (C. Basiliano)

1989

Right: With The Rolling Stones at Shea Stadium, October 1989. (Joel Levy/Starfile)

JOURNEYMAN
UK Duck Records WX322 926 074-1
US Duck Records 26074
Released November 1989

Side One:
1. Pretending
2. Anything For Your Love
3. Bad Love
4. Running On Faith
5. Hard Times
6. Hound Dog
Side Two:
7. No Alibis
8. Run So Far
9. Old Love
10. Breaking Point
11. Lead Me On
12. Before You Accuse Me

SEPTEMBER 1989
18
Stephen Bishop releases his 'Bowling In Paris' LP. Eric plays on 'Hall Light' which dates back to the 'Behind The Sun' sessions.

28
Da Campo Boario, Rome.
Joins Zucchero Sugar Fornaciari for a version of 'Wonderful World'. Other guests at this concert include Clarence Clemons, Paul Young and Dee Dee Bridgewater. The whole concert is shown on Italian TV.

OCTOBER 1989
7
Eric joins Elton John at Madison Square Garden in New York for 'Rocket Man'.

10
Eric joins The Rolling Stones at New York's Shea Stadium for 'Little Red Rooster'.

Eric Clapton: The song I played was 'Little Red Rooster' and I remember being taught how to play it by Howlin' Wolf himself 'cause we did an album together in London ('The London Howlin' Wolf Sessions') and it was quite a hairy experience. He came over and got hold of my wrist and said, "You move your hand up HERE!"

19
Eric joins The Rolling Stones at the Los Angeles Coliseum for 'Little Red Rooster'.

20, 21
Eric films the video for 'Pretending' in Los Angeles.

25
Eric records a TV special with David Sanbourn at New York's Rockefeller Centre. They perform two takes of 'Hard Times', 'Old Love' and 'Before You Accuse Me'.

28
Eric and Pete Townshend are interviewed together on Sue

Lawley's *Saturday Matters*. They perform a great acoustic version of Muddy Waters' 'Standin' Around Cryin'.

NOVEMBER 1989
6
'Journeyman' released.

Eric Clapton: I think it changed a little bit in the making. Pretty early on into the sessions we found that the material we were looking for would end up being like rock 'n' roll material. When we did 'Hard Times' I said, "This is the kind of album I want to make" and Russ Tuitleman said, "Well, let's do that . . . definitely." Given the fact that he made that smash hit album for Steve Winwood, I wanted to give him his head too. We agreed to postpone a blues album until our next project.

13
Polygram UK release a special 'Collector's' CD box set of '461 Ocean Boulevard', 'Timepieces' and 'Slowhand' along with a booklet.

17

EC/David Sanbourn TV Special broadcast in USA.

18

Royal Albert Hall, London.

Eric plays 'Edge Of Darkness' with the Organic Symphony Orchestra conducted by Michael Kamen. Eric is introduced by George Harrison and is supported by Andy Newmark on drums and Ray Cooper on percussion. The event is in aid of Parents For Safe Food.

Eric, along with George Harrison and Jeff Lynn, join Dame Edna Everage for the chorus of 'Why Do We Love Australia'.

The show also featured Wayne Eaglin and members of the Royal Ballet, Pamela Stephenson and Billy Connolly. The entire performance is filmed.

20

Phil Collins releases his 'But Seriously' album. Eric plays on 'I Wish It Would Rain' and appears in the video for this song.

26

Eric attends Tina Turner's 50th birthday party celebrations at The Reform Club in London's St James.

DECEMBER 1989
8, 9

Eric Records *Communion* film soundtrack at Townhouse Studios, London.

19

Convention Centre, Atlantic City, N.J.

Eric joins The Rolling Stones for 'Little Red Rooster' and 'Boogie Chillin'' also featuring John Lee Hooker. The whole concert is broadcast live on pay-per-view TV.

23

Eric joins Gary Brooker's 'No Stiletto.Shoes' band for a special Christmas show at Chiddingford Ex-Serviceman's Club.

Top: (Marc Roberty)

Centre: With George Harrison at JFK Airport, New York. (Mike Wherman/Starfile)

Bottom: With Jack Bruce, Bottom Line Club. (Michael Pawlyk/Starfile)

1990

Far right: (Philip Ollerenshaw/
Starfile)

Right: (Scott Firth/Retna)

JANUARY 1990
14, 15, 16

NEC, Birmingham. Start of UK tour.

These three shows were performed by the 'Four Piece Band' (Eric, Steve Ferrone on drums, Nathan East on bass and Greg Phillinganes on keyboards) and the set comprised 'Pretending', 'I Shot The Sheriff', 'Running On Faith', 'Breaking Point', 'Can't Find My Way Home', 'Bad Love', 'Lay Down Sally', 'Hard Times', 'Before You Accuse Me', 'No Alibis', 'Old Love', 'Tearing Us Apart', 'Wonderful Tonight', 'Cocaine', 'Layla', 'Crossroads', 'Sunshine Of Your Love'.

17

BBC Theatre, Shepherds Bush, London.

Eric and band perform 'Bad Love' on the *Wogan* TV show.

18, 19, 20, 22, 23, 24

Royal Albert Hall, London.

Six further shows by the 'Four Piece Band' with a set comprising 'Pretending', 'Running On Faith', 'Breaking Point', 'I Shot The Sheriff', 'White Room', 'Can't Find My Way Home', 'Bad Love', 'Lay Down Sally', 'Before You Accuse Me', 'No Alibis', 'Old Love', 'Tearing Us Apart', 'Wonderful Tonight', 'Cocaine', 'Layla', 'Crossroads', 'Sunshine Of Your Love'.

'Same Old Blues' was added to the programme on the 22nd, and on the 24th Phil Collins joined the band for an encore of 'Knockin' On Heaven's Door'. The show on the 24th was filmed and recorded.

26, 27, 28, 30, 31

Royal Albert Hall, London.

Eric leads a 13-piece band for these shows. They comprise Phil Palmer on guitar, Nathan East on bass, Greg Phillinganes and Alan Clark on keyboards, Steve Ferrone on drums, Ray Cooper on percussion, Katie Kissoon and Tessa Niles on backing vocals, and Ronnie Cuber, Randy Brecker, Louis Marini and Alan Rubin on horns.

The set comprised 'Pretending', 'Running On Faith',

HARVEY GOLDSMITH BY ARRANGEMENT WITH ROGER FORRESTER PRESENTS

ERIC CLAPTON

RECORD BREAKING
18 NIGHTS

THE ROYAL ALBERT HALL

JAN 18, 19, 20, 22, 23, 24, 26, 27, 28, 30, 31, FEB 1
WITH HIS BAND

FEB 3, 4, 5
AN EVENING OF THE BLUES WITH SPECIAL GUEST

FEB 8, 9, 10
AN EVENING WITH
THE NATIONAL PHILHARMONIC ORCHESTRA
WITH MICHAEL KAMEN

TICKETS £...

ROYAL ALBERT HALL

STALLS
DOOR 4   HARVEY GOLDSMITH & ROGER FORRESTER PRES
ROW G9   ERIC CLAPTON - A BLUES EVENING
SEAT 13   PLUS SUPPORT
092289   SUNDAY   FEB. 04/90 AT 7:30 PM
PRICE   EVENING
17.50   DOORS OPEN 45 MINUTES BEFORE PERFORMANCE
1-ZZ   ZZ
3-050508   PROMOTER
TO BE RETAINED SEE REVERSE FOR CONDITIONS OF SALE

Top: (Bob Gruen/Starfile)

Centre and bottom: (Joel Levy/Starfile)

'Breaking Point', 'I Shot The Sheriff', 'White Room', 'Can't Find My Way Home', 'Bad Love', 'Lay Down Sally', 'Before You Accuse Me', 'Old Love', 'No Alibis', 'Tearing Us Apart', 'Wonderful Tonight', 'Cocaine', 'Layla', 'Crossroads', 'Sunshine Of Your Love'.

FEBRUARY 1990
1

Royal Albert Hall, London. Performance as above, which was filmed and recorded.

3

Royal Albert Hall, London.
The first of the 'Blues Nights' on which Eric headed a band comprising Robert Cray on guitar and vocals, Buddy Guy on guitar and vocals, Johnnie Johnson on piano, Jamie Oldaker on drums and Robert Cousins on bass. The concert was divided into three

sections, Eric leading the first before handing over the show to Robert Cray and Buddy Guy.

Eric's set comprised 'Key To The Highway', 'Worried Life Blues', 'All Your Love', 'Have You Ever Loved A Woman' and a medley of 'Standing Around Crying' and 'Long Distance Call'; with Robert Cray leading, the band performed 'Going Down Slow', 'You Belong To Me', 'Cry For Me', 'Howling For My Baby' and 'Same Thing'; and with Buddy Guy leading, the band performed 'Money (That's What I Want)', 'Five Long Years', 'Everything's Gonna Be Alright', 'Something On Your Mind', 'My Time After A While', 'Sweet Home Chicago', 'Hoochie Coochie Man' and 'Wee Wee Baby'.

The whole concert was broadcast live on BBC Radio One FM.

4
Royal Albert Hall, London.

The second 'Blues Night' with the band as above and a set comprising 'Key To The Highway', 'Worried Life Blues', 'Watch Yourself', 'Have You Ever Loved A Woman', 'Johnnie's Boogie', 'Standing Around Crying'/'Long Distance Call', 'Going Down Slow', 'You Belong To Me', 'Cry For Me', 'Howling For My Baby', 'Same Thing', 'Money (That's What I Want)', 'Five Long Years',

'Something On Your Mind', 'Everything's Gonna Be Alright', 'Sweet Home Chicago', 'My Time After A While'.

5
Royal Albert Hall, London.

The third 'Blues Night' with the band as above and 'Wee Wee Baby' added to the set list. This show was filmed and recorded.

8, 9, 10
Royal Albert Hall, London.

For these 'Orchestral' shows

Eric led an eight-piece band accompanied by the National Philharmonic Orchestra conducted by Michael Kamen. The band was the same as January 26 less the horn section. The set comprised 'Crossroads', 'Bell Bottom Blues', 'Lay Down Sally', 'Holy Mother', 'I Shot The Sheriff', 'Hard Times', 'Can't Find My Way Home', 'Edge Of Darkness', 'Old Love', 'Wonderful Tonight', 'White Room', 'Concerto For Electric Guitar And Orchestra', 'Layla', 'Sunshine Of Your Love'.

The show on February 9 was

1990

filmed and recorded while the show on February 10 was broadcast on Radio One FM.

Eric Clapton: I'm very grandiose, so I decided that this year's project had to be a really mammoth production. I've always been susceptible to classical music, and I thought it would be nice to have a concerto not just for a guitar but for *my* guitar.

14

Icehall, Helsinki, Finland.

16

The Globe, Stockholm, Sweden.

17

Skedsmo Hall, Oslo, Norway.

19

KB Hall, Copenhagen, Denmark.

20

Sporthalle, Hamburg, West Germany.
   Rock Steady broadcasts part of Eric's 'Blues Night' from February 5.

22

Forest National, Brussels, Belgium.

Far right: (Mike Guastella/Starfile)

Right: (Pictorial Press)

Below: With the Royal Philharmonic Orchestra at London's Royal Albert Hall. (Marc Roberty)

23

Grughalle, Essen, West Germany.
   Ray Cooper injured his hand at this show and was unable to continue with the tour.

24

Statenhal, The Hague, Holland.

26, 27

Palatrussardi, Milan, Italy.

MARCH 1990
1

Olympiahalle, Munich, West Germany.

3, 4

Zenith, Paris, France.

5

Festhalle, Frankfurt, West Germany.
   The set for the European tour comprised 'Pretending', 'No Alibis', 'Running On Faith', 'I Shot The Sheriff', 'White Room', 'Can't Find My Way Home', 'Bad Love', 'Before You Accuse Me', 'Old Love', 'Tearing Us Apart', 'Wonderful Tonight', 'Cocaine', 'Layla', 'Crossroads', 'Sunshine Of Your Love'.

24

Eric appears on *Saturday Night Live* on US TV performing 'No Alibis', 'Pretending' and 'Wonderful Tonight' with his band. After the cameras stopped rolling Eric jammed with the Saturday Night band, performing 'Born Under A Bad Sign' and 'Hideaway'.

28

Start of American tour
   The Omni, Atlanta, Ga.
The band is the same as for the European dates, and the set normally comprises 'Pretending', 'Before You Accuse Me', 'Running On Faith', 'I Shot The Sheriff', 'White Room', 'Can't Find My Way Home', 'Bad Love', 'Lay Down Sally', 'No Alibi', 'Old Love', 'Tearing Us Apart', 'Wonderful Tonight', 'Cocaine', 'Layla', 'Crossroads', 'Sunshine Of Your Love'.

30

Coliseum, Charlotte, S.C.

31

Dean Smith Centre, Chapel Hill, N.C.

APRIL 1990
2

Madison Square Garden, New York, N.Y.
   Daryl Hall joins Eric for 'No Alibis'.

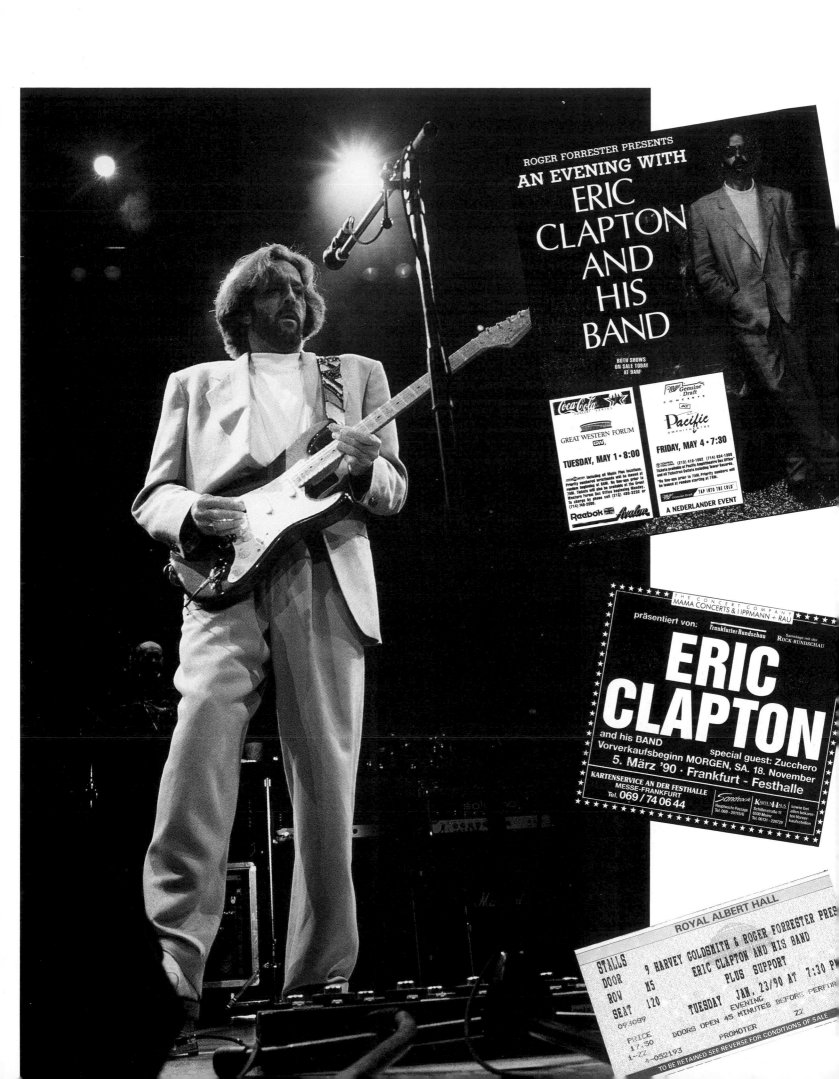

3

Meadowlands, Rutherford, N.J.

4

Spectrum, Philadelphia, Penn.

6

Coliseum, Nassau, Uniondale, N.Y.

7

Carrier Dome, Syracuse, N.Y.

9, 10

Centrum, Worcester, Mass.

12, 13

Civic Centre, Hartford, Conn.

15

Palace of Auburn Hill, Detroit, Mich.
    Stevie Ray Vaughn jams on 'Before You Accuse Me' and 'After Midnight'.

16

Riverfront Coliseum, Cincinnati, Oh.

17

Coliseum, Richfield, Minn.

19

Market Sq. Arena, Indianapolis, Ind.

20

Hilton Coliseum, Ames, Oh.

21

The Arena, St. Louis, Mo.

23

Lakefront Arena, New Orleans, La.

24

The Summit, Houston, Tx.

25

Reunion Arena, Dallas, Tx.

27

McNichols Arena, Denver, Co.

29

Tingley Coliseum, Albuquerque, N.M.

30

ASU Pavilion, Phoenix, Ar.

MAY 1990
1

Forum, Los Angeles, Ca.
    George Harrison joins Eric for 'Crossroads' and 'Sunshine Of Your Love'.

3

Sports Arena, San Diego, Ca.

4

Pacific Amphitheater, Costa Meso, Ca.

5

Shoreline Amphitheater, San Francisco, Ca.

JUNE 1990
6

Eric attends the Elvis Awards at the New York Armoury.

30

Knebworth.
    Plays in supergroup with Mark Knopfler and Elton John.

POSTSCRIPT

At time of going to press Eric was due to go back to the USA in July and August for more dates including some with Robert Cray and Stevie Ray Vaughn. South America, Japan and Australia were also strong possibilities. In January and February 1991, Eric will be back for his regular series of concerts at the Albert Hall for at least 24 nights, after which he is due for a well deserved year off.

On the record and video front, the next couple of years will see a double album from the Albert Hall 1990 shows, a newly remastered 'Layla' with unreleased jams, a 'Rainbow '73, Vol 2', 'EC Was Here, Vol 2' plus various collections of unreleased material, a new blues album and a possible John Mayall 'Bluesbreakers' album. There will also be a video from the Royal Albert Hall 1990 shows.

Far left, top: (Zoran Veselinovic/Retna)

Far left, centre: (Pictorial Press)

Far left, below: With Elton John. (LFI)

Left, top: (LFI)

Left, centre: (LFI)

Left, below: (Joel Levy/Starfile)

Overleaf: (Philip Ollerenshaw/Starfile)